MW00877091

The
1031
SOLUTION

EXCHANGE YOUR REAL ESTATE
FOR OIL & GAS ROYALTIES

DIRK TODD

The 1031 Solution, Exchange Your Real Estate
for Oil & Gas Royalties
Copyright © 2014 Dirk J. Todd
ISBN 978-1-304-86982-1

All rights reserved. No part of this book shall
be reproduced, stored in a retrieval system, or
transmitted by any means, electronic, mechanical,
photocopying, recording, or otherwise, without
written permission from the publisher. No patent
liability is assumed with respect to the use of the
information contained herein. Although every
precaution has been taken in the preparation of
this book, the publisher and author assume no
responsibility for errors or omissions. Nor is any
liability assumed for damages resulting from the use
of the information contained herein.

Printed in the United States of America

First Printing: January 2014

Trademarks

All terms mentioned in this book that are known
to be trademarks or service marks have been
appropriately capitalized. Madison Business
Books, LLC cannot attest to the accuracy of this
information. Use of a term in this book should
not be regarded as affecting the validity of any
trademark or service mark.

Warning and Disclaimer

Every effort has been made to make this book
as complete and as accurate as possible, but no
warranty or fitness is implied. The information
provided is on an "as is" basis. The author and
the publisher shall have neither liability nor
responsibility to any person or entity with respect
to any loss or damages arising from the information
contained in this book.

Cover Designer:
Sarah E. Mathewson
Book Layout and Design:
Sarah E. Mathewson
Copy Editor:
Sarah E. Mathewson

Printing and Binding
Lulu Press

Published by
Madison Business Books LLC
402 Gammon Place, Suite 200
Madison, Wisconsin 53719

ISBN
978-1-304-86982-1

DIRK TODD
about the author

Dirk Todd is regarded as one of the preeminent authorities on 1031 Exchange strategies utilizing energy royalty and mineral interests. His first book, *Stomp the IRS Out of Your Capital Gains* (2009), expounded upon many of his previously published articles on the subject.

As president and founder of the private equity firm, Madison Capital Investments LLC, the author has spent his career specializing in passive income strategies, energy investments and 1031 exchange replacement acquisitions. As a nationally-recognized advisor on these subjects, he is often invited to speak at events throughout the U.S.

It was through these types of engagements that he came to realize there existed a widespread misunderstanding of oil and gas royalties, as well as a lack of awareness of their eligibility as "like kind" property for 1031 exchanges.

His latest book, *The 1031 Solution*, seeks to rectify this issue. Written specifically for real estate investors, it covers the basics of the oil and gas industry and explores the benefits and risks involved in investing in energy royalties. With the help of industry experts, he discusses the elements and tax implications of a 1031 exchange and outlines proven strategies for diversification and maximizing tax deferral using royalty and mineral replacement properties.

The author grew up in central Texas and attended the University of Texas for 3 years before earning his bachelor's degree from Ohio University. He holds an MBA from Capital University. He was appointed by Governor Jim Doyle to the Wisconsin State Advisory Board for the Department of Financial Institutions where he served for 3 years. He and his family currently reside in southern Wisconsin with another residence in Dallas, Texas.

ROBBY BARNES
oil & gas royalty expert

Robby Barnes is a partner in Madison Capital, LLC. He manages the Dallas office and is responsible for business development and capital raising efforts across MCI's various channels of distribution.

Mr. Barnes has extensive experience in royalties and alternative investments. He has been involved in the acquisition and divestiture of more than twenty private royalty offerings, which have raised in excess of $300 million.

A fifth generation Texan and son of a petroleum engineer, Mr. Barnes was introduced to the oil and gas industry at an early age and purchased his first royalty deal in 2002. He grew up in Plano, Texas and attended Texas Tech University. He now lives in Frisco, Texas with his wife and two sons.

CRAIG BROWN, ESQ.
qualified intermediary

Craig Brown, Esq., IPX1031® vice president and regional manager, has overseen the facilitation of 5,000 plus exchanges of real and personal property with total values in excess of $3 billion.

He has trained over 7,500 attorneys, CPAs, Realtors® and escrow officers on like-kind exchanges and works with specialty divisions and general counsel for parking title exchanges and multiple asset exchanges. Craig develops and teaches like-kind exchange continuing education training in-house and is a frequent speaker for legal, real estate and tax associations.

KIM JAMES
financial & operations executive

Kim James is a senior financial & operating executive with experience in both publicly traded and entrepreneurial manufacturing companies ranging in size from $10 million to $3.2 billion. Mr. James has a broad range of industry experience in consumer products, beverage, pharmaceuticals, flavor, animal health, chemicals, and agribusiness and has a reputation for developing solutions to complex financial and business situations and implementing initiatives that improve value and operating results.

Mr. James has a BS in Business Administration with High Distinction from the University of Arizona, did graduate work at Northwestern University, and is a CPA.

CONTENTS

THE 1031 SOLUTION

exchange your real estate for oil & gas royalties

ONE

"the best investment on earth is earth"

- Louis J. Glickman

If you own real estate investments, are you considering selling your property? Maybe you have grown tired of the ongoing expenses and maintenance associated with property ownership and the hassles of dealing with tenants, toilets, and trash; perhaps you're frustrated with the increasing regulation in the industry; or maybe it's just a good time to sell, and you're looking for alternatives to real estate that can add diversification to your portfolio. If so, this book was written for you. In it I present an investment alternative that is less management intensive and offers more potential cash flow—namely, oil and gas royalties. I will detail a strategy I've employed for years that will allow you to use the 1031 tax deferred exchange to trade some of your current real estate holdings for energy royalty interests. Among other benefits, these interests can provide long-term income while capitalizing on the growth of domestic oil and gas production.

The Purpose of This Book

Like many of you, I have been in the trenches of the real estate industry. I have been involved in numerous types of transactions, including triple net leases and tenants in common, as a buyer, seller, and broker. I owned multiple properties and was actively managing them when a close friend introduced me to oil and gas royalties over a decade ago.

To test the waters I decided to invest in a partnership that owned a small collection of domestic oil and natural gas royalty interests. I soon discovered that, while not perfect, these oil and gas interests offered some significant advantages that made them excellent additions to my portfolio of real estate. The more I learned, the more I was drawn to this uniquely-American asset class--so much so that my professional focus changed entirely.

Over time I came to realize that most owners of investment real estate are in the same position that I was those many years ago. They are unaware that the oil and gas royalties asset class even exists, let alone that these properties can be acquired through a tax-free 1031 exchange. Like me, many who learn about the benefits of this investment are eager to incorporate royalties into their own portfolio strategies and wish they had been exposed to this alternative investment sooner.

For example, one of my clients owned a number of multi-family properties and was planning to sell one of his apartment buildings. He had significant gain on the property and was looking at writing a sizable check to Uncle Sam. I explained how, instead, the client could exchange the apartment building for an investment in natural gas royalties and defer the tax liability on the sale. This strategy worked well within his portfolio since the royalties investment would provide a hedge against the rising utility costs on his remaining buildings. As his utility expenses increased due to a rise in the price of natural gas, so would the monthly checks he received from his investment in the royalties, either partially or fully offsetting his increased costs.

Maybe you are a real estate investor who is preparing to retire and would like to get out of the active management business and invest in something that will provide you with additional income for doing virtually nothing. If you sell your investment properties and have a capital gain, you'll have to pay taxes to the federal government, leaving you less to invest in something that will generate passive income. This 1031 exchange solution allows you to exchange your real estate for oil and gas royalties without the tax bite, giving you more money to invest, translating in many cases to larger monthly checks in the mailbox.

Exchanging real estate for oil and gas royalties offers numerous advantages, but, as with any investment, you have to know what you're doing

in order to make wise investment decisions--which is why I decided to write this book. I wanted to be able to reach more people to introduce them to this alternative and educate them on the best ways to use the distinctive characteristics of energy royalties to complement their existing real estate portfolios through a 1031 transaction.

What Sets This Book Apart

Although numerous books have been written on the topic of 1031 exchanges, most of them tend to focus only on the IRS Code and the mechanics of the transaction. I have read many of these books and found them to be very good at explaining the basic concept and the technicalities involved. I wrote *The 1031 Solution: Exchange Your Real Estate for Oil and Gas Royalties* to go well beyond that, however.

This book not only introduces the basics of a 1031 exchange, but also presents an analysis of the tax implications of not executing an exchange. It will provide a general overview of what royalty interests are and how they are generated. And I share details on the investment strategies my firm uses to acquire royalty interests for our clients as well as our own portfolio to provide the reader with a thorough comprehension of how oil and gas royalties can be used effectively in a 1031 exchange.

Another unique feature of this book is that certain topics are presented by an expert in the respective field. I have gathered a team of accomplished professionals, all with extensive experience, to assist me in the writing of this book. Each of these men draws on his particular expertise to provide readers with a clear understanding of all aspects of a 1031 exchange into oil and gas royalties. My co-author, Mr. Robby Barnes, is a partner in Madison Capital, the private equity company I founded in 2007. A fifth generation Texan and son of a petroleum engineer, he is intimately familiar with the gas and oil industry and has been involved in the acquisition and divestiture of over $300 million in private royalty offerings. Craig Brown, Esq., a qualified intermediary (QI) who has overseen the facilitation of more than 5,000 exchanges and develops and teaches courses on like-kind exchanges, introduces the fundamental elements and mechanics of a 1031 exchange. To provide insight on the tax implications of a sale of property and the financial impact of reinvestment, I've brought in Kim James, a CPA and senior financial executive who has built a distinguished career providing financial analysis and direction to companies undertaking takeovers, bankruptcies, asset liquidations, stock buy-backs and complete corporate restructuring.

In addition, we provide the reader with some insight into the dynamic, ever-changing world of energy. Madison Capital has been actively engaged in the purchase of oil and gas royalties for the last several years, and our team has carefully studied the market in the process of doing so. In this book I share our analysis of the energy industry, including current trends and future predictions, to provide readers with a better understanding of the benefits and risks of this alternative asset class. I explore the technological advances in drilling that have opened up billions of dollars in future oil and gas reserves, making millionaires—virtually overnight—of mineral and royalty owners throughout the country.

The U.S. oil and gas industry is experiencing unprecedented production growth and because of the unique access private citizens have to mineral ownership, it is my opinion that there has never been a greater opportunity for investors to participate in direct ownership of oil and gas wells. My hope is that you will enjoy this book and use the information provided to profit from our domestic energy resources by exchanging your real estate for oil and gas royalties.

TWO

inside the 1031 exchange

I n this chapter I enlisted the expertise of Craig Brown, Esq., a foremost authority on the structure and process of a 1031 exchange. As a Qualified Intermediary, Craig has facilitated more than 5,000 such exchanges, serving as an independent party to the exchange transactions. He shares his expert and detailed knowledge of the exchange process with you in the following pages. This chapter will serve as a refresher for those needing to brush up on the fundamentals and mechanics of a 1031 exchange.

What is a 1031 Exchange?

A 1031 Exchange is a tax-deferred exchange of like-kind property, authorized by Section 1031 of the Internal Revenue Code (IRC). Specifically, the code states:

No gain or loss shall be recognized on the exchange of property held for productive use in a trade or business or for investment if such property is exchanged solely for property of like kind which is to be held either for productive use in a trade or business or for investment.

One of the most important phrases in the above statement is "like kind." To qualify for tax-deferred exchange treatment under IRC 1031, the relinquished property must be exchanged for replacement property that is of "like kind." The Internal Revenue Service (IRS) recognizes two primary property classes—real and personal. And, to quote a famous poet, never the twain shall meet; real property and personal property are never viewed as "like kind." But let's consider each of these two property classes in more detail.

Real property is defined as land and includes the rights and interests to the natural resources contained on or in the land, such as timber, coal, oil and gas, and any immovable structures attached to it. Despite its name, personal property does not necessarily mean property used by an individual in a personal capacity. Rather, personal property includes all property that is not considered real property. This said, although the 1031 tax-deferred exchange is authorized by federal statute, individual state laws dictate whether the property to be exchanged is considered real or personal.

In real property exchanges, the term "like kind" refers to the nature or character of the property and not to its grade or quality. [*Treas. Reg. 1.1031(a)-1(b)*] For example, it doesn't matter whether the property is unimproved or improved--vacant land or an apartment building--because that reflects only the grade or quality, not the property kind or class. In essence, all real property is considered to be "like kind" by the IRS. A single-family rental is considered "like kind" to an apartment building, a commercial building, and even to a mineral or royalty interest.

Tax-deferred exchanges involving personal property are a bit more challenging. The relinquished and replacement properties must be in either the same general asset class or the same product class. An airplane is not "like kind" to office furniture, and light general purpose trucks are in a different asset class from heavy general purpose trucks. We will elaborate on this point in the section on personal property exchanges. But for now let's examine some of the other wording in the statement taken from Section 1031 of the IRC more closely.

To qualify for a tax-deferred exchange, the relinquished property must have been held as an investment or "for productive use in trade or business," and the replacement property must also be held as an investment or for productive use in the exchanger's trade or business. In other words, even though both your personal residence and a commercial building are classified as real property and, as such, are "like kind," you cannot exchange your personal residence for a small storefront using a 1031 exchange since your personal residence is not used primarily for trade or business purposes.

However, if you own a single-family rental and wish to exchange it for a more passive investment in real property, such as a royalty interest, you can do so under Section 1031 of the IRC and avoid paying capital gains taxes. "No gain or loss shall be recognized on the exchange" since both the relinquished property and its replacement are held for investment purposes.

Excluded Properties

Not all properties can qualify for a 1031 exchange, however. Section 1031 specifically excludes the following:

- Stock in trade or other property held for the purpose of resale (i.e., inventory, which includes property held by a developer or other dealers in property)
- Stocks, bonds, or notes
- Other securities or evidences of indebtedness or interest
- Partnership interests [*Note: the partnership can elect out of partnership status under IRC 761(a).*]
- Certificates of trust or beneficial interests
- Choses in action (i.e., the right to receive money or other personal property enforceable only by judicial proceeding)

In addition, the IRS has ruled that the following exchanges don't qualify under §1031 of the IRC:

- Oil payments up to a defined dollar amount for an overriding royalty reserved from the same lease [*Midfield Oil Co. v. Commissioner 39 B.T.A. 1154 (1939)*]
- Transfer of all mineral interest excepting out a ¼ royalty for farm land [*Crooks v. Commissioner, 92 TC816 (1989)*]

Furthermore, intangible drilling costs must be recaptured if qualified natural resource properties are not acquired in an exchange.

Real Property Exchanges

When most people purchase real estate, they receive what is termed as a fee simple interest—or fee interest—in the property. This means they have absolute ownership of the land and everything on and below the land. This fee interest is not the only interest in real property that you can purchase, however. A fee interest owner can sell part of his ownership rights—such as the rights to the minerals lying beneath the land--to others. As alluded to earlier, these lesser ownership interests are generally considered to be real property and thus meet the like-kind requirement to serve as a replacement property for investment real estate in a 1031 exchange. The IRS will look to state law to determine whether the specific interest is treated as real property or personal property. [*Aquilino v. United States, 363 U.S. 509 (1960)*] Examples of these include:

- A remainder interest in realty;

- Cooperative apartments, when they are considered equivalent to real estate under state law, as is the case in California;

- Mineral rights, water (riparian) rights, scenic easements, agricultural conservation easements, and possibly air rights, development rights and zoning rights (which must be considered real estate under state or local law to qualify as an interest in real property); and

- Timber rights.

To expound on this last item, standing timber is considered an interest in real property in some states and can therefore be exchanged for any other interest in real property, such as an apartment complex or a retail mall. [*Anderson v. Moothart, 198 Or. 354, 256 P.2d 257 (1953) and Cary A. Everett,[m1] T.C.M. 1978-531*] However, if the timber is being sold subject to a cutting contract, which requires that the timber be removed from the land within a reasonable time, it might be considered a personal property interest under applicable state law and, thus, not be of "like kind" to real property for 1031 exchange purposes. A personal property exchange is still possible, but the replacement property can only be cut timber. [*Oregon Lumber Company v. Commissioner, 20 T.C. 192 (1958)*]

There are also certain types of real property ownership on which the IRS has issued rulings that are particularly pertinent:

Leasehold Interests

A lease with 30 years or more remaining, including renewal options, is considered to be "like kind" to a fee interest in real estate, while a lease with a term of less than 30 years is not. [*Century Electric Co. v. C.I.R., 192 F.2d 155 (8th Cir. 1951); Treas. Reg 1.103(a)-1(c); and Rev. Rul. 78-72, 1978-1 C.B. 258*]

A "carve out" of a lease interest does not qualify as like-kind property, either. Therefore, a fee owner of real property cannot exchange a "carve out" 30-year lease in a property for a fee interest in a replacement real property. [*Rev. Rul. 66-209, 1966-2 C.B. 299*] This is in contrast to an exchange of real property that is "subject to" a long-term lease. The latter is treated as real property for the purposes of qualifying for an exchange since the lessor has a reversionary interest—i.e., ownership of the property may revert back to the lessor under certain conditions. [*Rev. Rul. 76-301, 1976-2 C.B. 241*]

Undivided Interests

Another issue arises when there is a partition of property among co-owners or when co-owners of the same property wish to exchange their undivided interest in the whole property for an exclusive fee interest in a portion of the same property. Assume, for example, that you and a group of friends decided to pool your monies to purchase a small condominium complex at a ski resort, and each of you obtained an undivided interest in the whole property but then later wished to exchange your individual undivided interests in the whole for exclusive fee interests in one of the units of the complex. Happily, these transactions have been allowed and have received favorable exchange treatment by the IRS. [*Rev. Rul. 79-44, 1979-1 C.B. 265; Rev. Rul. 73-476, 1973-2 C.B. 301*]

The IRS has also issued guidance for reviewing the viability of using a 1031 exchange to acquire a tenancy in common (or fractional ownership) interest in a replacement property in which there are a large number of co-tenants in a co-tenancy arrangement. [*Rev. Proc. 2002-22*] The main issue for the IRS is that the large number of co-tenants in the replacement property may cause the ownership structure to be re-characterized as a partnership, and partnership interests do not qualify for 1031 exchanges, as noted earlier in this section.

Mixed Uses

In many cases, real property is held for a number of reasons—investment, personal use, resale, or productive use in trade or business. In these situations, the exchanger should seek tax and legal advice because it is necessary to allocate the sale and purchase prices to the appropriate qualified and non-qualified property portions of the exchange. In Sayre v. U.S., 163 F. Supp. 495, the court ruled that any reasonable allocation would be acceptable.

The property need not be surveyed or partitioned to achieve this. An allocation could be determined, for example, with an appraisal based upon the number of units or the relative square footage of the units. Nevertheless, bear in mind that the proceeds from the sale of the qualified exchange portion of the relinquished property must be used to purchase qualified replacement property. None of it can go toward the purchase of whatever portion of the replacement property will be used for personal purposes or it will be taxable as "boot," as will be explained shortly.

For example, assume an exchanger relinquishes the family homestead and the surrounding ranch—a mix of personal and business use. He can take advantage of the principal residence capital gains tax exclusion (subject to specific limitations) under IRC 121 and simultaneously execute an exchange on the ranch portion of the property under IRC 1031. The replacement property could be a single property consisting of another personal residence with a ranch or two separate properties, such as a single-family home and an apartment complex.

Boot

We're not talking about footwear here. "Boot" refers to items of personal property and/or cash that are used to even out an exchange--property that is received in an exchange that is not "like kind" to the other property acquired in the exchange transaction. The use of boot in a transaction does not totally disqualify the exchange for tax-deferred treatment, but an exchanger generally must recognize a taxable gain in the amount of the fair market value of the boot received. Common examples of boot are:

- Cash proceeds an exchanger receives from the Qualified Intermediary during or after the exchange;
- Nonqualified property, such as stocks, bonds, notes, or partnership interests;
- Proceeds received in the form of a note or contract for sale of the property; (An exchanger can utilize IRC 453 to recognize the gain (boot) of a seller carry-back note received in an exchange transition under the installment sale rules.)
- Relief from debt, either on the relinquished property (due to an assumption of the mortgage, trust deed or contract) or on the replacement property when debt on it is paid off as part of the exchange;
- Personal property received in the exchange;
- Property intended for the exchanger's personal use and not for investment or business purposes.

To avoid receiving boot—and the resultant tax consequences--the exchanger must be sure to:

1. Purchase like-kind replacement property of equal or greater value (i.e., net sales price) to the relinquished property;
2. Use all the net equity (exchange funds) from the sale of the relinquished property to purchase the replacement property; and
3. Finance the replacement property with an equal or greater amount of debt than was paid off, assumed, or taken "subject to" on the relinquished property.

Personal Property Exchanges

As mentioned earlier, personal property is all property that is not considered real property, with the distinction left to the individual states. Personal property can be further classified as tangible or intangible.

Tangible personal property refers to things such as cars, trucks, and planes, while intangible property includes assets like franchise rights, copyrights, and broadcast spectrums. Examples of the types of personal property that qualify for a 1031 exchange include:

Airplanes	Coin Collections
Helicopters	Fleets of Automobiles
Barges	Trailers and Containers
Buses	Office Furniture
Copyrights	Construction Equipment
Franchises	Agricultural Equipment
Artwork	Restaurant Equipment
Trucks	Broadcast Spectrums

Most tangible personal property used in a trade or business is depreciable, meaning you can deduct the cost of the item for tax purposes over a certain period of time. In contrast, as a general rule, the cost of intangible assets cannot be written off unless they were acquired through the purchase of a substantial portion of a business.

Depreciable Tangible Assets

To be of "like kind," depreciable tangible personal property must be in either the same General Asset Class or the same Product Class. This means that sometimes multiple exchanges must be executed—one for each

separate asset class. For example, in an exchange involving a hotel, a lot of personal property may be included—furniture, computer equipment, restaurant equipment—all of which are categorized in different classes. The General Asset Classes for depreciable tangible personal property are as follows:

- Office furniture, fixtures, and equipment
- Data handling equipment (computers not included)
- Information systems (computers included)
- Airplanes (commercial passenger and freight carriers not included) and helicopters
- Automobiles (including taxis)
- Buses
- Light general purpose trucks
- Heavy general purpose trucks
- Railroad cars and locomotives
- Tractor units
- Trailers and trailer-mounted containers
- Vessels, barges, tugs (excluding those used in marine construction)
- Industrial steam and electric generation and/or distribution systems

The Product Classes for depreciable tangible personal property are defined by Division D of the Standard Industrial Classification Manual of 1987. (In fact, this is the only purpose the manual serves these days.) There are cases wherein a depreciable tangible personal property item is not included in either a General Asset Class or a Product Class, however. A tax-deferred exchange is still possible, as long as the relinquished and replacement properties are deemed to be "like kind."

Non-Depreciable Tangible Personal Property and Intangible Personal Property

This also applies to non-depreciable tangible personal property and intangible personal property. There are no specific classes provided for these types of assets, so in order for a 1031 exchange to take place, the exchanged properties must be considered to be "like kind." There are some rules provided for general guidance. As one example, livestock of different sexes is not considered like-kind property.

The like-kind test for intangible personal property lies in the "nature or character of the rights involved" and also in the "nature or character of the underlying property to which the intangible personal property relates," according to the IRS. Therefore, a copyright on a novel can be exchanged for a copyright on another novel, but it cannot be exchanged for a copyright on a song and qualify for tax-deferment. A novel and a song are not considered like-kind properties.

It is important to note that the goodwill of one business is never considered "like kind" with the goodwill of another business. Therefore, goodwill is not 1031-exchange eligible.

It is strongly recommended that anyone wishing to conduct a 1031 personal property exchange seek the services of a tax advisor. Among other things, a good tax professional can help the exchanger determine the respective property values and the purchase and sales prices for each element involved in the transaction.

Calculating Deferrable Gains

The goal of a Section 1031 exchange is to defer taxes on any capital gains that would otherwise result from the sale of an asset. Therefore, an understanding of how the taxable gain on the sale of an asset is determined is essential to understanding the concept.

The total price that must be paid to acquire an asset is its initial cost basis, or tax basis. For example, if you purchase a truck using $10,000 cash-in-hand and a $30,000 loan, its initial tax basis is $40,000. As mentioned earlier, the cost of most tangible personal property used in a trade or business must be depreciated over time; you cannot deduct the entire cost of the asset for tax purposes in the year that you purchase it.

The percentage of the cost of a depreciable asset that is tax deductible each year is determined by the IRS and depends on the type of property. For example, a truck is classified as 5-year property by the IRS, which means it can be depreciated over 5 years to a tax basis of zero using either straight-line depreciation or the Modified Accelerated Tax Recovery System (MACRS), under IRC 168. (For those of you who are accounting types, we're ignoring the half-year convention for simplicity reasons.) If straight-line depreciation is used, the owner can write off 1/5-- or 20%--of the initial cost of the truck each year. This means that by the end of year 3, the owner will have written off 60% of the cost of the truck, or $24,000, making its adjusted basis $16,000.

The MACRS schedule allows for a faster write off: 20% in year 1; 32% in year 2; 19% in year 3; 11.52% in years 4 and 5; and 5.76% in year 6 if the asset is still owned. Thus, by the end of year 3, the accumulated depreciation on the truck would amount to 71% of its initial cost, or $28,400, leaving an adjusted basis of $11,600.

At any given point in time, the adjusted basis of the asset is equal to its original cost minus the accumulated depreciation that has been taken over the years, plus any capital improvements made to the asset. (We essentially assumed no capital improvements in the truck examples presented above.) And it is the adjusted basis that is used to determine the taxable gain when the asset is sold. Using our truck example and MACRS depreciation, if the owner were to sell the truck at the end of 3 years for a net price of say, $16,000, he would have a taxable gain of $16,000 - $11,600 = $4,400. The gain is simply the net selling price minus the adjusted basis. This is the amount we would target to defer when executing a 1031 exchange. When dealing with non-depreciable tangible assets or non-amortizable intangible assets, the adjusted basis will be the initial tax basis plus the cost of any improvements to the asset.

As another example, assume an airplane is acquired for $120,000. This is its initial tax basis. Airplanes are classified as 7-year property by the IRS. Using the MACRS schedule for 7-year property, at the end of 2 years it will have been depreciated by 38.77% ($46,524) to a value of $73,476. But assume that during these 2 years, avionic upgrades valued at $20,000 have been added to the plane. The adjusted basis at the end of the 2 years is, therefore, $120,000 - $46,524 + $20,000 = $93,476.

As noted above, we subtract the adjusted basis from the net selling price to determine the taxable gain, if any. If the result is negative, it is a loss that can be used to offset capital gains from other sources. If it is positive, it is necessary to determine what portion of the gain is attributable to the depreciation taken on the asset during the years of ownership and what portion is the result of appreciation in the value of the asset since the two may be taxed at different rates.

To illustrate, let's assume an automobile is purchased for business use at a price of $38,000 and is sold at the end of 3 years for $24,000. Although its initial cost basis was $38,000, it was depreciated by $28,500 over the 3-year period, leaving an adjusted basis of $9,500. The taxable gain is $24,000 - $9,500 = $14,500, all of which is the result of the depreciation write-off since the car sold for less than its original value. In essence, the car was depreciated to a value of $9,500, but its value was actually $24,000 at the end of the 3 years, as indicated by its selling price. This gain is taxable as something called a "recapture of depreciation" since the depreciation deductions taken exceeded the actual deterioration in the value of the vehicle. Assuming a 35% tax rate for depreciation recapture, the taxpayer would owe 0.35 x $14,500 = $5,075 in taxes on the sale of the vehicle. This may not seem like much, but consider that leasing companies and other businesses that utilize large fleets of automobiles acquire and dispose of thousands of vehicles per year. This can result in a huge tax liability. Firms that utilize tax-deferred exchanges as part of their tax planning strategy benefit from significant tax savings.

Like-Kind Properties

It is impossible to provide a complete list of like-kind properties, but a number of exchange examples are provided below to give you an idea of the realm of possibilities. I have provided references to the specific rulings for some of them for those of you who are interested in exploring the details of the particular exchange further.

- Residential for commercial real estate
- Vacant land for rental real estate
- Fee simple interest in real estate for a 30-year leasehold
- Single-family rental for multi-family rental
- Non-income producing raw land for income-producing rental property
- Rental mountain cabin for a dental office in which the Exchanger intends to practice
- Corporate twin-engine aircraft for a corporate jet
- Mitigation credits for restoring wetlands for other mitigation credits
- Buses for buses

- Garbage routes for garbage routes

- Foreign real property for foreign real property

- Livestock for livestock of the same sex (Note: livestock of different sexes are not considered "like-kind.")

- Mineral estate for an undivided interest in a city lot [*Commissioner v. Chrichton, 122 F2nd 181 (5th Cir. 1941)*]

- Oil lease extending until exhaustion for fee interest in an improved ranch. [*Rev. Rul. 68-331*]

- Overriding royalty for unimproved real estate [*§1033 issue. Rev. Rul. 72-117*]

- Royalty interest for real estate [*PLR 7935123, 7935126, 8135048*]

The Mechanics of a 1031 Exchange

There is a general misconception that all tax-deferred exchanges are complicated and require all properties—the relinquished and the replacement—to close concurrently. Nothing could be further from the truth. There are a number of ways a 1031 exchange can be effected:

- Swap
- Buyer-facilitated 3-party
- Seller-facilitated 3-party
- Qualified Intermediary (QI) Simultaneous
- QI Delayed
- QI & Exchange Accommodation Titleholder (EAT) Relinquished Parked (Reverse)
- QI & EAT Replacement Parked (Reverse)
- QI & EAT Build-to-Suit (BTS)
- QI & EAT Replacement Parked BTS (Reverse BTS)

The most common of these is the delayed exchange—also referred to as a "deferred" or "Starker" exchange. [*Starker v. U.S. 602 F.2d 1341*] We will, therefore, focus most of our discussion of the mechanics on it.

The Delayed Exchange

The delayed exchange offers the exchanger greater flexibility and more options for acquiring the replacement property than does the simultaneous exchange. The delayed exchange is initiated with the sale of the first relinquished property and ends when the last replacement property is acquired within the prescribed exchange period. Both the sales contract for the relinquished property and the purchase contract for the replacement property should include an "exchange cooperation" statement to provide the legally required notice to the parties involved.

The Role of a Qualified Intermediary

The services of a Qualified Intermediary (also known as an "accommodator" or "facilitator") are used to complete a valid delayed exchange quickly and easily. As an independent party to the exchange transaction, the Qualified Intermediary performs a number of functions. He creates the reciprocal trade of the properties, holds the exchange funds, and prepares the requisite documentation, including the exchange agreement and assignments and closing instructions.

PARTIES INVOLVED IN AN EXCHANGE

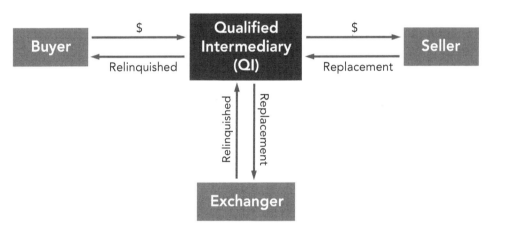

The Exchanger assigns the rights to the relinquished and replacement properties to the Qualified Intermediary in the sales (relinquished) and purchase (replacement) contracts, effectively making the Qualified Intermediary the seller of the relinquished property and the buyer of the replacement property. When the relinquished property is sold, the proceeds are held by the Qualified Intermediary until they are needed for the acquisition of the replacement property. This enables the Exchanger to avoid actual or constructive receipt of the exchange funds, as required by §1031 of the IRC.

When a Qualified Intermediary is used to create the reciprocal exchange of properties, the IRS allows "direct deeding" of the relinquished property from the Exchanger to the buyer and of the replacement property from the seller to the Exchanger. [*Revenue Procedure 90-34, 1990.16 C.B. 552 Treas. Reg. 1.1031(k)-1(g)(4)(v).*] This avoids the necessity of having the Qualified Intermediary take title of the properties, which, in turn, avoids the assessment of double state, county or local documentary transfer taxes. It also relieves the Qualified Intermediary of any liability for environmental hazards that may exist on the property. Direct deeding is possible in both simultaneous and delayed exchanges that use a Qualified Intermediary.

Delayed Exchange Deadlines and Identification Requirements

When executing a delayed exchange, it is critical that the replacement property be properly identified within the specified identification period and acquired by the end of the exchange period. Regulations issued by the U.S. Treasury Department in 1991 clarified the acceptable methods for properly identifying replacement property. [*Treas. Regs. 1.1031(k)-1(b) through (e)*] It is essential to follow the rules and meet the deadlines set forth. Failure to comply may result in a failed exchange.

There are two key deadlines that must be met for a delayed exchange to be valid, as defined by the identification period and the exchange period:

1. Identification Period: The Exchanger has 45 days from the sale of the first relinquished property to properly identify potential replacement properties. The replacement property must be acquired by the end of the exchange period.

2. Exchange Period: The Exchanger must receive the replacement property no later than

   a. 180 days from the date on which the Exchanger transferred the first relinquished property, or

   b. the due date (including extensions) of the Exchanger's tax return for the tax year in which the transfer of the first relinquished property occurs whichever comes earlier.

These deadlines are very strict and cannot be extended--even when the

45th day or the 180th day falls on a Saturday, Sunday, or legal holiday. There are two acceptable methods for identifying the replacement property. The first is simply to purchase the replacement property within the time frame of the identification period. The second is to identify the property in a written document (the "Identification Notice"), sign the document, and deliver it to a party directly involved in the exchange by midnight of the 45th day after the sale of the first relinquished property. Parties directly involved in the exchange include the seller of the replacement property, the Qualified Intermediary, an escrow, settlement or title officer, or a person who is providing the Exchanger with services solely related to the exchange of the property.

1031 EXCHANGE TIMELINE

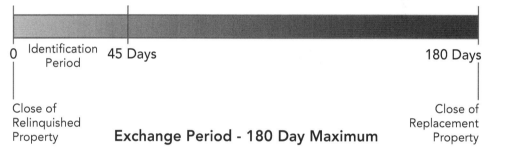

The Identification Notice

The Identification Notice must contain an unambiguous description of the replacement property and, as noted earlier, must be signed by the Exchanger. A fully executed purchase and sale agreement specifying the replacement property can satisfy these requirements. Barring that, the legal description, street address, or distinguishable name must be provided for real estate. Moreover, if the Exchanger intends to improve the replacement property within the time frame of the exchange period, an adequate description of the underlying land and a description of the proposed construction or improvements must be provided in as much detail as is practicable at the time the Identification Notice is prepared. When identifying replacement property in a real property exchange, any personal property included in the purchase that has a value of less than 15% of the total value of the replacement property is considered incidental and does not need to be identified.

Exchangers are afforded the flexibility of identifying more than one property as a potential replacement property for the exchange. The three rules governing this are as follows:

1. Three Property Rule: This allows the Exchanger to identify any three properties as potential replacement properties, without regard to fair market value.

2. 200% Rule: The Exchanger may identify any number of properties as potential replacement properties, provided that the aggregate fair market value of all the identified properties does not exceed 200% of the aggregate fair market value of all the relinquished properties on the date of their transfer.

3. 95% Exception: If the Exchanger identifies more potential replacement properties than allowed under either the Three Property or 200% Rules, the Exchanger must receive, by the end of the exchange period, replacement property that has a fair market value of at least 95% of the aggregate fair market value of all the identified replacement properties. The fair market value is determined by the property value on either the date the Exchanger receives the property or the last day of the exchange period, whichever is earlier, without regard to any liabilities secured by the property.

The Identification Notice for replacement property can be revoked any time prior to the end of the Identification Period if the Exchanger opts not to purchase that particular property for exchange purposes. The revocation must be done in writing, signed by the Exchanger, and delivered to the same party who received the original Identification Notice.

Multiple Asset Exchanges

In many cases, an Exchanger owns an asset that consists of both real and personal property, as is the case with a hotel or a restaurant. This creates some additional issues that need to be addressed. For one thing, the assorted assets must be allocated to the correct like-kind category, using a property-by-property comparison. Additionally, the deferred gain and basis must be allocated among the various exchanged assets. An Exchanger can often realize a greater benefit by utilizing a multiple asset exchange structure than by executing separate exchanges for each type of asset.

The IRS had initially issued a ruling that stated that an exchange of the identical business assets of two telephone companies—both real and personal property—would be considered "property of like kind" within the framework of IRC 1031. [*Rev. Rul. 57-365*] However, in 1989, a new rule, Rev. Rul. 89-121, sought to clarify the "identical business asset" rule set forth in Rev. Rul. 57-365. The new rule stated that the mere fact that multiple assets comprise a business or integrated economic investment does not necessarily allow them to be regarded as the disposition of a single property. Instead, a review of the underlying assets pursuant of Rev. Rul. 55-79 would be required to determine whether the property would be considered "like kind." Accordingly, pure "business swaps" are a thing of the past.

The current system for tax-deferred exchanges applies to all transactions occurring on or after April 11, 1991. It requires all Exchangers contemplating a multiple asset exchange to group the properties, both real and personal, into like-kind or like-class groups. [*Treas. Reg 1.1031(j)-1*] While this may not sound much different from what must be done when using a separate exchange for each property, multiple property exchanges do provide an exception to the general rule requiring a property-by-property comparison when computing the gain and basis.

Although the assets must be segregated into exchange groups containing like-kind properties, the values and liabilities associated with the individual units are computed in aggregate, and a gain is recognized for an exchange group only to the extent of a difference in these aggregate values. [*Treas. Reg. 1.1031(j)-1(b)*] The computation of the resulting basis remains unchanged, however; the basis is determined separately for each exchange group. [*Treas. Reg. 1.1031(j)-1(c)*] The end result is an exchange of multiple properties that allows a greater proportion of the gain to be deferred than had separate exchanges been executed.

As mentioned earlier in this chapter, it is important to remember that the goodwill or "going concern" value of one business is not of "like kind" to the goodwill or "going concern" of another business. The rationale provided for this ruling is that the goodwill or "going concern" value of two businesses could not possibly have the same nature or quality. Thus, an exchange of "Tony's Pizza of NY" for "Joe's Pizza of SF" can consist only of the real property and equipment. The value of Tony's goodwill, which very well may represent the bulk of the value of the business, real property excepted, is not eligible for tax-deferred exchange treatment.

When you think about it, a lot of commercial real property transactions include a large amount of depreciated personal property that is sold along with the real property. If an Exchanger takes the time to review the situation and investigate the possibility of a multiple property exchange in these instances, he will often find he can defer much more of the taxable gain than he thought possible. Multiple asset exchanges are complex, however; exchangers are strongly advised to obtain competent tax and legal counsel prior to the exchange.

Related Party Exchanges

Although exchanges between related parties are allowed, the Exchanger must adhere to specific rules for the exchange to qualify for tax-deferred treatment. Internal Revenue Codes 267(b) and 707(b)(1) define a related party as any person or entity bearing a relationship to the Exchanger, such as family members (brother, sister, spouse, ancestors, and lineal descendants); a grantor or fiduciary of any trust; two corporations that are members of the same controlled group; or corporations and partnerships in which the same persons own more than 50% of the value of the outstanding stock of the corporation and more than 50% of the capital interest or profits interest in the partnership.

IRC 1031(f) makes it clear that two related parties owning separate properties may "swap" those properties with one another and defer the recognition of any gain as long as both parties hold their replacement properties for at least 2 years following the exchange. This rule was imposed to prevent taxpayers from using exchanges to shift the tax basis between the properties for the sole purpose of tax avoidance.

More typical related-party exchanges are executed via a Qualified Intermediary (QI). Either the Exchanger transfers the relinquished property to the QI in return for replacement property previously owned by a related party, or the QI sells the Exchanger's relinquished property to the related-party buyer. There is some uncertainty regarding the treatment that these types of related-party exchanges will receive from the IRS. Most tax advisors agree that exchanges in which the Exchanger sells relinquished property to a related-party buyer through a QI have a better chance of qualifying for a tax deferral, but only if both the buyer and the Exchanger hold the exchanged properties they receive for 2 years. However, Rev. Rul. 2002-83 stipulates that tax-deferred treatment will be denied to an Exchanger who acquires replacement property previously owned by a related party from a QI if the related-party seller receives any cash or other non-like-kind property in payment, regardless of how long the replacement property is held. The IRS generally views this latter transaction as the same as if the Exchanger had swapped properties with a related party who then immediately sold the property acquired, in violation of the 2-year holding period requirement.

In fact, IRC 1031 (f)(4) stipulates that a related-party exchange will be disallowed if it "is a part of a transaction (or series of transactions) structured to avoid the purposes of § 1031 (f)(1)," i.e., the related-party provisions. An exception to the 2-year holding period requirement is allowed if the subsequent disposition of the property is due to (1) the death of the Exchanger or related person or (2) the compulsory or involuntary conversion of one of the properties under IRC 1033, assuming the exchange occurred prior to the threat of conversion. Barring these, if the Exchanger can establish that neither the exchange nor the disposition of the property was done to avoid taxes, any gains will still be tax-deferred.

It is also important to note that under IRC 1031 (g), the 2-year holding period is "tolled" for the period of time during which (a) either party's risk of loss on their respective property is diminished because the party owns a put, giving him/her the right to sell the property; (b) either property is subject to a call, which gives a 3rd party the right to purchase the property being held; or (c) either party engages in a short sale or any other similar transaction involving the property. Any one of these three scenarios stops the clock insofar as the 2-year countdown is concerned.

As you might have ascertained in reading this section, related-party exchanges can be confusing. And there are many other important issues regarding them that are not clearly defined by the IRS—issues that can have varying tax consequences. The Exchanger should seek tax or legal counsel to weigh the risks involved.

Planning for the Exchange

Any 1031 exchange transaction requires additional preparation, expertise, and support to be successful. Your Qualified Intermediary will typically handle the exchange details, documentation, and safeguard the exchange equity. Nevertheless, you should confirm some facts and answer some questions yourself prior to initiating a tax-deferred exchange. This will help you avoid unnecessary obstacles that can sometimes occur and make the process go more smoothly. The following checklist is designed to get you started:

- ☑ Confirm that the property you are selling (the relinquished property) has been held as a rental or investment property and that you intend to do the same with the replacement property.

- ☑ Ensure that the title to the replacement property will be held in the same manner as the title on the relinquished property.

- ☑ If borrowing funds to purchase the replacement property, confirm that the lender has no specific requirements for holding title that would pose a problem for the exchange.

- ☑ Determine if you will need to use any of the sales proceeds to make cosmetic or structural improvements to either the relinquished or replacement property.

- ☑ Consider the various types of exchanges that you can use to meet your exchange objectives—e.g., simultaneous, delayed, build-to-suit, and reverse—and decide which one best fits your needs.

- ☑ Answer the following questions:

  1. Will part of the proceeds be used to pay personal debt?

  2. Will additional parties be added to the title of the replacement property?

  3. Will all members on the title to the relinquished property be participating in the exchange?

  4. Are you selling any property to or intending to buy property from a related party?

5. Do you plan to offer seller financing on the sale of the relinquished property? *Maybe*

I've no doubt that some of the material covered in this chapter will seem daunting if this is your first introduction to it. However, I've also no doubt that you will find the tax savings and lifestyle benefits that you will enjoy by learning more about 1031 exchanges and how they can be used effectively to convert your active investments in real property to less time-consuming, passive investments well worth your effort.

THREE

selling real estate: a tax reality

P resident Theodore Roosevelt said, "In any moment of decision, the best thing you can do is the right thing. The worst thing you can do is nothing." In respect to this idea, I wanted to include a chapter that discussed how a real estate investor might evaluate the options available to him in determining what to do with the proceeds from the sale of investment property, specifically, whether or not a tax deferred exchange is the "best thing" for his situation.

Since a decision like this attaches a tax implication to each investment option, and since I am neither a CPA nor a financial advisor, I have recruited a friend who is much more qualified than myself to present this discussion. Kim James is a CPA who has spent his career helping companies navigate complex financial decisions through comprehensive analysis. I anticipate you will find his professional insight in the following pages to be equally intriguing as it is informative.

The 1031 Exchange Opportunity

Successful investors understand the importance of carefully analyzing the financial aspects of a transaction, including the opportunity costs and tax implications involved, when weighing investment alternatives. This chapter will focus on the tax treatment of 1031 exchanges and illustrate some of the advantages of executing one of these "like-kind" exchanges. Bear in mind that the discussion that follows is just an overview of some of the state and federal tax consequences. It should not be construed as tax or legal advice. Tax laws can and do change, and taxes are just one piece of any investment decision. Investors are encouraged to seek the advice of a certified public accountant (CPA) or qualified financial advisor who understands their financial, tax and risk mitigation objectives and how those may be impacted by specific investment alternatives.

Section 1031 of the Internal Revenue Code provides investors with a unique opportunity to avoid paying taxes on gains incurred with the disposition of real estate. Specifically, Section 1031 allows real estate investors to defer--or postpone--capital gains on an investment property when all of the proceeds of the sale are invested in a "like kind" investment: "No gain or loss shall be recognized on the exchange of property held for productive use in a trade or business or for investment, if such property is exchanged solely for property of like-kind which is to be held either for productive use in a trade or business or for investment." IRC §1031(a)(1).

Moreover, there is no limit to the number of times an investor can execute a 1031 exchange, deferring taxes with each transaction. Nor will you be leaving your heirs with a tax liability. As the law is currently written, when an investor defers the payment of capital gains taxes through a 1031 exchange--or multiple 1031 exchanges--his or her heirs will receive a stepped-up basis upon the death of the investor. In other words, an investor can defer until he dies, and no capital gains tax will be owed by his heirs.

Tax Consequences of a Sale vs. an Exchange

The potential tax liability resulting from the outright sale of real estate can be significant. Any gain on the sale is taxed at the federal level, and investors in most states must pay taxes to the state as well. Investors with higher levels of taxable income are also subject to the newly instituted Section 1411 Medicare surtax on investment income. Furthermore, any depreciation that was taken on a property that sells for more than its depreciated value (i.e., its net adjusted basis) is "recaptured" since the property clearly did not depreciate by that amount. Currently, the maximum tax rate levied on the recaptured amount is 25%.

Calculating the Realized Gain on a Sale

The first step in determining the taxes due upon the sale of real estate is calculating the realized gain. This is the amount by which the selling price exceeds the net adjusted basis of the property. The calculation involves 2 simple steps:

1. Determine the net adjusted basis of the property by adding the cost of any capital improvements to the original purchase price of the property and subtracting the total of all depreciation taken over the years of ownership.

2. Calculate the realized gain by subtracting the sum of the net adjusted basis and any commissions and fees incurred in the sale from the selling price of the real estate.

For example, assume an investor purchased some rental property 10 years ago for $350,000 and has made $90,000 in improvements to it over the years. Assume, too, that she has claimed a total of $100,000 in depreciation on her tax returns. If she sells the property today for $650,000 and pays $40,000 in commissions and fees related to the sale, her realized gain will be $270,000, calculated as follows:

Net adjusted basis	=	purchase price	+	cost of improvements	-	depreciation
$340,000	=	$350,000	+	$90,000	-	$100,000

Realized gain	=	selling price	-	(adjusted basis	+	fees & commissions)
$270,000	=	$650,000	-	($340,000	+	$40,000)

Calculating the Taxes Due

If the property has been held for more than 1 year, the resultant gain will be taxed at the investor's long-term capital gains tax rate, which is based on his level of taxable income. (If the property has been held for less than a full year, the gain will be taxed at the same rate as the investor's ordinary income gets taxed, which, in most cases, is much higher.) As mentioned above, a Medicare surtax may also apply. The 2013 federal rates are provided in the table below:

Single Taxpayer	Married Filing Jointly	Long-term Capital Gain Tax Rate	Section 1411 Medicare Surtax	Combined Tax Rate
$0 - $36,250	$0 - $72,500	0%	0%	0%
$36,250 - $200,000	$72,500 - $250,000	15%	0%	15%
$200,000 - $400,000	$250,000 - $450,000	15%	3.8%	18.8%
$400,001+	$450,001+	20%	3.8%	23.8%

State capital gain tax rates vary from 0% to 11%, with a national average of about 5%, and an investor may also be subject to local taxes on the sale in some cases. For example, the city of New York levies a tax on capital gain income.

The depreciation recapture must also be factored into the equation. Thus, the total tax liability associated with the sale of a property is the sum of 4 elements:

- the recapture of the depreciation, which is determined by multiplying the total depreciation taken by the recapture rate;

- the federal tax on the capital gains, which equals the realized gain multiplied by the long-term capital gain tax rate;

- the Medicare surtax, if applicable, which is calculated by multiplying the realized gain by the 3.8% surtax; and

- state and local taxes on the sale, if applicable. These are calculated by multiplying the realized gain by the appropriate tax rate.

So, to continue with our example, let's assume our investor has taxable income of $300,000 and must pay a 25% depreciation recapture tax and 5% in state taxes on the sale. Based on the information in the table above, she will pay federal tax on the gain at the rate of 15% and will also be subject to the Medicare surtax. If she sells the property outright, realizing a gain of $270,000, she will pay over $89,000 in taxes on the sale, as calculated below:

Depreciation Recapture	=	0.25	x	$100,000 (total depreciation)	=	$25,000
Federal tax on realized gain	=	0.15	x	$270,000	=	$40,500
Medicare surtax	=	0.038	x	$270,000	=	$10,260
State tax on realized gain	=	0.05	x	$270,000	=	$13,500
Total Taxes Due						$89,260

If instead, the investor had executed a 1031 exchange, she would have had $89,260 more to invest in the new asset since a like-kind exchange is not a taxable event, and the taxes can be deferred indefinitely.

As you might surmise from the preceding discussion, the total tax liability on the sale of real estate can vary greatly depending on the investor's taxable income, the adjusted basis of the relinquished property, and the tax laws of the state. In some instances it can be as high as 35% of the realized gain.

Weighing the Alternatives

As another example, assume that an investor has been offered $1.5 million for an investment property that he originally purchased for $500,000. Over the years, he made $50,000 in capital improvements on the property and claimed a total of $80,000 in depreciation deductions on his tax returns. His 2013 taxable income is $500,000. He has decided to dispose of the property, but wants to consider the available alternatives, including investing in a new, larger property with the proceeds. He also wants to analyze how doing a 1031 exchange for the new property might benefit him if this is the route he decides to take.

One of the first things he will need to know is how much he will have to invest in an alternative asset if he sells the existing property outright rather than doing a 1031 exchange. Using the information provided and the 2013 federal tax rates in the table, we can calculate the taxes he will owe:

Original Purchase Price	$500,000
Add: Capital Improvements	$50,000
Less: Depreciation	$80,000
Net Adjusted Basis	**$470,000**
Sales Price	$1,500,000
Less: Net Adjusted Basis	$470,000
Less: Sales Expenses (8%)	$120,000
Realized Gain	**$910,000**
Recaptured Depreciation (25% x depreciation taken)	$20,000
Federal Capital Gains Tax (20% x realized gain)	$182,000
Medicare Surtax (3.8% x realized gain)	$34,580
State Capital Gains (5% x realized gain)	$45,500
Tax Liability	**$282,080**

In this example, a 1031 exchange will save the seller $282,080. The tax on the gain will be deferred, leaving him with more funds available to invest in a like-kind property, as illustrated below:

	1031 Exchange	No 1031 Exchange
Sale Price	$1,500,000	$1,500,000
Less: Sales Expenses	$120,000	$120,000
Less: Taxes	$0	$282,080
Net Proceeds	**$1,380,000**	**$1,097,920**

And the more money he has to invest, the greater his future annual cash flow will be, all else equal, as the table on the following page shows:

Rate of Return						
Amount Invested	6%	8%	10%	12%	14%	16%
$1,380,000	$82,800	$110,400	$138,000	$165,600	$193,200	$220,800
$1,097,920	$65,875	$87,834	$109,792	$131,750	$153,709	$175,667

Note that the seller will have to earn more than 10% (10.055%, to be exact) on his new investment if he opts not to do a 1031 exchange in order to generate the same annual cash flow he would earn if he had used a 1031 exchange to invest in another piece of real property with an expected return of only 8%. And as any good investment advisor will tell you, higher expected returns come with higher levels of risk.

Looking at it from another angle, we can see that if the new investment property provides an annual return of 14%, the seller will earn almost $40,000 a year more on his investment if he does the exchange ($193,200 vs. $153,709) simply because the 1031 exchange enables him to invest more money in the new property than he would have had available had he sold his existing property outright and used the after-tax proceeds to invest in the new asset.

Of course, additional analysis is needed to ensure the investor makes the value-maximizing choice. For example, the availability of desirable new properties and the management and maintenance a new, larger property will require must be considered, along with the cost and process for obtaining any debt financing needed. The flexibility provided by a 1031 exchange and the amount of the sale proceeds that will need to be invested to meet the requirements of a 1031 exchange and defer the taxes associated with the sale must also be examined. And the investor should consider whether he should reduce the percentage of real estate holdings in his investment portfolio and diversify into other types of assets that offer the desired return.

Regardless of the type of alternative asset being contemplated, the investment analysis must consider the investor's objectives and constraints and should include:

■ the funds available for reinvestment;

■ the return that is needed to meet his financial goals and the expected return on the new investment;

- his level of risk aversion and the risk associated with the new investment;

- his investment horizon and exit strategy;

- his liquidity needs;

- his tax status and the tax treatment of the investment return; and

- its impact on his overall investment portfolio and estate plan, including any diversification potential that the new asset will provide.

Additional considerations are the management costs the investor will incur in terms of money, time, and effort and what he could earn on alternative investments of similar risk (i.e., his opportunity cost).

Obviously, there are any number of investment alternatives that could be considered should the real estate investor elect to pay capital gain tax on the sale of his investment property. Still, the ability to defer $282,080 in taxes and invest those funds in a qualified investment is a significant opportunity. While the taxes deferred lower the basis of the new investment and are essentially paid when the investment is liquidated, the basic fact that a dollar today is worth more than a dollar in the future provides a significant benefit. And the longer the payment is deferred and the higher the investor's opportunity cost, the greater is the value of being able to do so.

The table below illustrates what a future payment of $282,080 is equal to in terms of today's dollars, given the number of years the payment is deferred and some hypothetical alternative annual rates of return that might be earned on those deferred tax dollars.

Number of years payment is deferred	Hypothetical average annual rate of return on $282,080				
	6%	8%	10%	12%	14%
5	$210,787	$191,979	$175,149	$160,060	$146,504
10	$157,512	$130,658	$108,754	$90,822	$76,089
15	$117,702	$88,923	$67,528	$51,535	$39,518
20	$87,954	$60,520	$41,929	$29,242	$20,525

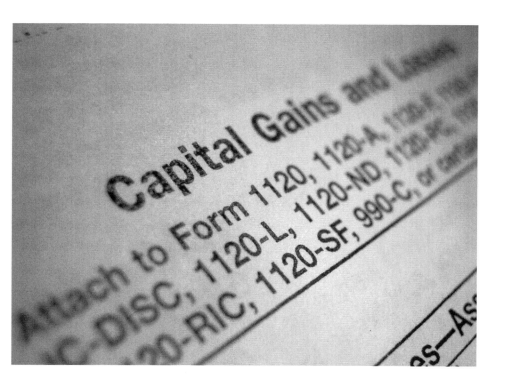

In other words, if the seller can defer payment of the $282,080 in capital gains taxes for 20 years and can earn an average annual return of even just 6% on that money, the money he will pay to the government 20 years from now will be equivalent to paying only $87,954 in today's dollars. Said another way, if the seller were to set aside $87,954 today in an account that earns 6% a year compounded, in 20 years he would have the $282,080 to pay the taxes he deferred today.

The ability to leverage the equity by deferring taxes to future years allows the investor to earn returns on the money rather than writing a check for taxes. Moreover, a real estate investor can continue to keep this equity invested by structuring 1031 exchanges on all future property sales as well. This tax strategy provides the opportunity for tax-deferred growth and the potential to increase investor net worth over time through the acquisition of larger properties or multiple properties that produce greater cash flow.

Acquiring a property by executing a 1031 exchange can also be an effective estate planning strategy. To reiterate a point made earlier, when the investor passes away, the basis of the properties he owned will be adjusted to reflect their fair market value at the time of his death. Thus, his heirs could, if they wanted, sell the properties immediately without incurring any depreciation recapture or capital gain tax on the sale.

Some Final Caveats

The preceding analysis has been designed to illustrate only the general principles and benefits of a 1031 Exchange. It is a relatively simple example used to highlight some of the steps investors should take to evaluate their options when selling investment real estate. The examples in this chapter are hypothetical scenarios based on existing tax laws. Each individual needs to understand and complete an analysis based on his specific tax situation, including the impact of any net operating losses he may have and his state's tax treatment of real estate transactions. It's also important to remember that IRS guidelines and federal and state tax rates are not set in stone. Changes in any of these elements can have a significant impact on the analysis, as can new tax court rulings.

Furthermore, as mentioned at the beginning of this chapter, tax is only one element in the analysis of any potential real estate transaction. A complete analysis should, at a minimum, include the following:

- an outline of the key financial facts, including the available alternatives;

- a purposeful identification of the investment strategy, including the targeted return and maximum level of risk desired;

- a risk assessment of the alternatives;

- the diversification potential of each of the alternatives;

- the investor's cost of capital;

- the actual cash impact of the transaction, which should consider the time value of money—i.e., $1 in the investor's pocket today is worth more than $1 he receives in the future;

- the tax implications of the alternatives being considered, including opportunities to minimize taxes;

- The ability to obtain debt and service any debt associated with the transaction as well as the potential impact debt holders can have on operations due to debt covenants and reporting requirements;

- The costs associated with executing the transaction and managing the investment, including the costs of both time and money;

- the expected returns and risk levels of alternative investments and the management process required to achieve those returns.

If necessary, you should consult a CPA or financial advisor for help in conducting a complete analysis based on your specific investment profile.

OIL & GAS
101

FOUR

oil & gas 101

There are two types of rights attached to land ownership—surface rights and mineral rights. In most countries, a landowner has only surface rights, which are the rights we typically associate with owning land, e.g., the rights to farm or ranch the land and/or erect buildings on it; the government retains the mineral, or subterranean, rights, which include the rights to any minerals and/or oil and gas that exist on or beneath the earth's surface. The United States is one of only a handful of countries in which a private property owner has both rights. This full and absolute ownership of the land is known as a "fee simple estate," which can be separated into two distinct estates: a surface estate and a mineral estate.

Fee simple estate title holders who have no interest in extracting whatever lies beneath the surface will sometimes sell the mineral rights to the land, retaining only the surface rights. Mineral estate owners possess legal title to the mineral deposits below the surface, e.g., coal, metal ores, and oil and natural gas. In many states, the mineral interest is considered "dominant," enabling mineral rights owners to use the surface estate to the extent reasonably necessary for the exploration, development and production of what lies below the surface.

Purchasers of these mineral estates are often speculators who have no intention of mining or drilling the land themselves. Instead, they hope to be able to sell or lease the rights to a company that is in the business of doing so. Oil and natural gas rights, the topic of this chapter, are typically leased. Mineral estate owners have what are termed "executive rights," which allow them to enter into a lease agreement with an operator/driller, transferring the right to extract the hydrocarbons believed to exist below the surface to the operator. This includes the right to build roads and facilities and drill wells.

THE BREAKDOWN OF RIGHTS AND INTERESTS

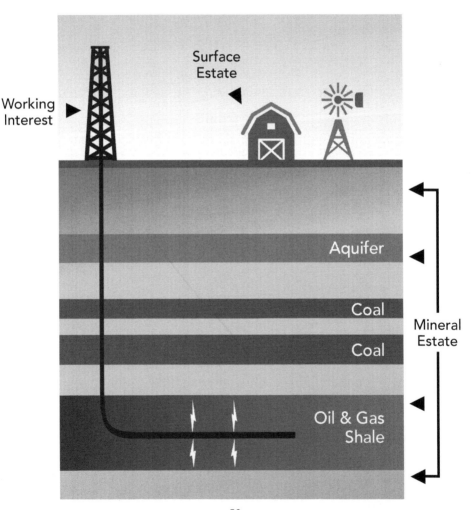

The lease agreement establishes two distinct ownership interests in the operational responsibilities and production revenues: a working interest and a royalty interest. The operator (lessee) and its investors are working interest owners. As such, they are collectively responsible for 100% of the drilling and operational costs and assume all liabilities. In return, they typically share in 75 to 87.5% of the production revenues after the royalty interest owners, i.e. the mineral rights owner(s) (lessor), are paid their royalties as stipulated in the lease agreement. This is usually between 18 to 25% of the production revenues. Some states set a minimum royalty percentage, often 12.5%. The mineral rights/royalty interest owners shoulder none of the drilling or production costs and are indemnified from any liabilities associated with the drilling operations.

The Drilling Process

To fully understand the concepts of working and royalty interests, you need to be acquainted with the drilling process itself. The timeline provided in this section will help.

Step 1: Prospecting

Geologists identify areas that they believe are good oil and gas production candidates, based on mapping, seismic interpretations, and information obtained from logs of surrounding wells.

Step 2: Drilling Lease

Once an area has been identified, the land department of the oil company searches the county courthouse records to determine who holds the title to the mineral rights of the land in question. The owner(s) is then contacted and an oil and gas lease detailing the rights of the operator and the royalties to be paid to the owner(s) is negotiated.

Step 3: Proposal to Drill

After the lease is acquired, an Authorization for Expenditure (AFE), a document that provides an estimate of the costs of drilling the well, is circulated to all working interest owners to raise the funds necessary to drill the well. All interest owners in the property are informed of the intent to drill, and legal title is prepared.

Step 4: *Survey and Permit*

A thorough survey of the drill site and surrounding area is completed. The company obtains a permit to drill from the state agency that oversees drilling activities.

Step 5: *Build Location*

Roads to the drill site are built. The drilling rig is positioned, and compensation is made to the surface rights owner for any surface damages.

Step 6: *Spudding*

"Spudding" is the term used to refer to the beginning of drilling a new well. Intermediate casings may be added along the way to stabilize the well bore as the well gets deeper, resulting in increased pressure.

Step 7: *Testing and Completion*

Geologists take core samples from the well bore to determine such factors as porosity, permeability, and pressure. Once testing

and drilling are complete, production casing is run the total depth of the hole and cemented in place. The drilling rig is disassembled, and the completion phase begins.

Step 8: Fracture Stimulation and Pipelines

After the cement of the production casing cures, a completion rig is moved in, and the well is hydraulically fractured. This enhances the permeability of the formation, allowing better flow of oil and gas to the well bore. Pipelines are then run to the wellhead, connecting it to the main gathering system in that area.

Step 9: Division Orders

The well operator prepares the Division Order, which notifies all interest owners that a new well has gone into production and stipulates the exact decimal interest of ownership. After all agree that the stated percentage ownership interests in the well are correct, the operator places each interest holder into pay status.

Step 10: Pay Status and First Check

The well begins to produce. Although the effective date is the first date of production, interest owners should not expect to see their first check for 60 to 90 days. The first 30 days are spent in the actual production. The oil and gas volumes are finalized, balanced, and recorded during the month after that. The purchasers of the oil and gas then pay the well operators, who must, in turn, distribute the money received to all the interest owners, based on the Division Order.

Working Interests: Benefits, Costs, and Risks

As noted previously, a working interest is a percentage ownership in an oil and gas lease that gives the owners the right to explore, drill, and produce oil and gas from a tract of property. Working interest owners have the potential to earn large returns, but they are also exposed to a considerable amount of risk.

Each working interest owner is responsible for paying a share of the cost of leasing, drilling, producing, and operating the well, based on the percentage ownership of the total working interest. In addition, before working interest owners can receive any income, royalties to the royalty interest owners must be paid, as specified in the lease agreement. Only then do working interest owners receive their proportional share of the remaining production value.

It is important to note that the percentage share of the production value to which a working interest owner is entitled will necessarily be less than the percentage share of the costs he is required to bear. To illustrate, assume that there is only one working interest owner and one royalty interest owner. Further assume that the negotiated royalty interest percentage is 12.5%. Remember that royalty interest owners pay none of the costs associated with the oil and gas production; those expenses fall entirely on the shoulders of the working interest owner(s). Thus, our solitary working interest owner will bear 100% of the production costs, but he must pay the royalty interest owner 12.5% of the production value, so he will receive only 87.5% of the production value himself.

Although major oil companies have the capital to fund the entire cost of drilling a well, they will sometimes sell non-operator working interests to investors. Non-operators are not involved in any way with the physical operation of the well, but they still must pay their fair share of the costs. Anyone considering the purchase of a non-operator working interest is advised to perform the necessary due diligence to determine the operator's financial standing prior to investing.

Smaller oil companies are known as "independents." Independents do not engage in wildcatting, a term which refers to the drilling of exploratory wells in hopes of discovering a new field. Instead, they choose to drill in existing fields. This allows them to study and analyze the logs of previous wells on the property to improve the likelihood of hitting a productive reservoir. These smaller firms often don't have the financial resources to carry them through a series of dry holes. If an independent doesn't feel capable of bearing the full financial risk of drilling, it will sell working interests in the well to investors and other independents. This enables it to spread their risk over more wells.

Benefits of Working Interest Ownership

There are a number of advantages to owning working interests, not the least of which is the ability to share in the largest portion of the revenue stream of a producing well. Although royalty interest owners receive their money first, working interest owners typically split 75 to 80% of the production revenue among themselves. Working interest owners usually get a higher return on their investment than royalty interest owners, which makes sense since they bear more of the risk.

The other advantages to working interest ownership come in the form of tax write-offs. Because working interest owners are considered to be active, rather than passive, investors, any profits or losses on their investment in oil and gas drilling programs are treated as "ordinary" by the Internal Revenue Service (IRS). It is considered to be income (or loss) from a trade or business, and the losses can be used to offset taxable income from other sources, such as salary or wage income. Moreover, working interest owners are able to deduct their share of both the intangible drilling costs (IDCs) and tangible drilling costs (TDCs) when calculating their taxes.

Intangible Drilling Costs (IDCs)

Intangible drilling costs are certain costs associated with the development and drilling of a well. These include survey and site preparation expenses and consist of items such as labor, chemicals, cement, grease, fuel, and repairs. These can range anywhere from 65 to 88% of the total cost of a well, and a working interest owner can deduct 100% of his share of these costs in the first year.

Thus, a $100,000 investment can result in a $65,000 to $88,000 reduction in taxable income in the initial year of the venture. Furthermore, this deduction can be taken in the year in which the investment was made, even if the drilling does not begin until the following year as long as it commences prior to the end of the 90th day after the close of the taxable year and certain other conditions are met. (See Section 461 of the Tax Code.)

Tangible Drilling Costs (TDCs)

Many of the costs of developing and drilling an oil or natural gas well- such as the cost of the equipment used- are treated as capital expenditures in the eyes of the IRS. This means that the working interest owner cannot deduct 100% of his share of the cost in the first year, but he can deduct his share of a certain percentage of the cost (i.e., the depreciation allowance) each year of the depreciable life of the asset. (See Section 263 of the Tax Code.)

You may be asking yourself why a cost-conscious Congress would provide such hefty tax breaks to the "Big Oil" working interest world--a very unpopular move from a political standpoint. The answer is risk. Congress recognizes the significant amount of risk involved in drilling an oil or gas well. The venture can easily result in either a dry hole or a poor-producing well. Congress also realizes the importance of fully developing our domestic oil and gas natural resources. Thus, Congress provides the IDC and TDC tax deductions to encourage the small and mid-sized producers to make this risky investment. The deductions help the working interest owners recover the costs incurred in drilling failed wells (dry holes) or marginal producers by allowing them to keep more of the revenues from a successful well.

Why then does Congress not provide the royalty interest owners with the same tax-deduction benefits? Again, the answer is risk—or the relative lack thereof. Recall that royalty interest owners bear none of the costs of drilling, completing, servicing, or maintaining the well. They simply own the mineral rights to the property. And in most oil and gas lease agreements, the mineral rights owner receives an upfront payment called a "lease bonus" or "advance royalty." This amount is negotiated and is paid by the mineral acre, based on the going rate in the area. Thus, the mineral rights/royalty interest owner doesn't face the economic risk that the working interest owners assume. No incentive is needed to get them to agree to lease their mineral rights in return for a royalty interest in the well.

Costs and Risks of Working Interest Ownership

As discussed previously, working interest owners are obligated to pay a percentage of all the costs associated with the drilling of a well, based on their proportionate ownership in the endeavor. In addition, the income earned by working interest investors is subject to the self-employment tax.

Self-Employment Tax

Self-employment tax is comprised of Social Security and Medicare taxes, those taxes that are withheld from the pay of most wage earners. Anyone with net earnings from self-employment exceeding $400 must pay this tax. In 2013, the self-employment tax rate was 15.3%; of this, 12.4% was for Social Security insurance (old-age, disability, survivors) and 2.9% was for Medicare (hospital insurance). The Medicare tax must be paid on 100%

of the taxpayer's net earnings, while there is a cap on the amount of earnings that is subject to the Social Security tax. This cap changes annually.

The employer-equivalent of the self-employment tax is deducted in calculating the taxpayer's adjusted gross income (AGI).

Production Risk

The Initial Potential Production (IPP) of a new well must be reported to the state oil and gas regulatory agencies. As the name implies, the IPP is simply a projection of the possible reserves in a given well. The IPP is oftentimes also provided to potential working interest investors. It is important to remember that the IPP may or may not be realized. One of the risks that working interest investors face is that actual production will not match IPP.

Insurance Risk

In most jurisdictions working interest owners are personally liable for any personal and property damages incurred. Responsible operators—i.e., those in charge of the actual physical operations of the project—maintain appropriate levels of insurance, but not all operators are responsible. Unforeseen and/or unfortunate events that result in personal or property damage during the development or production life of a well could exceed the level of insurance carried. This will result in reduced income for the working interest owners and, in some cases, the owners may have to pay additional monies from their own pockets. Bear in mind, too, that insurance may not cover pollution or other environmental problems that might result in personal or property damage.

Environmental and Regulatory Risk

Environmental liability statues are applicable to oil and gas operations. Environmental concerns, including the presence of endangered wildlife and the proximity of operations to public venues, can impede progress.

Joint and Several Liability Risk

Generally speaking, working interest owners are jointly and severally liable for obligations relating to operations. This means that an individual or entity can go after the owner(s) with the deepest pockets for the entire amount of any monetary claims it has, leaving those owners to seek restitution themselves from the remaining working interest owners. Furthermore, a working interest owner can remain liable in perpetuity for unforeseen events that occur both during the production life of a well and after it is plugged or abandoned.

Operator Risk

The operator is the entity that oversees the physical operations of the venture. Thus, the quality and experience, or lack thereof, of an operator can have a material effect on outcomes both during and after the drilling and completion of a well. As noted earlier, responsible operators will maintain adequate insurance; irresponsible ones may not. Additionally, an irresponsible operator may fail to pay subcontractors for work performed. These subcontractors can then file vendor liens on the well and any revenue it generates, thus preventing distributions to working interest owners until the bills are paid in full.

Many operators offer their services to working interest owners on a "turnkey" basis—i.e., at a fixed price. It is critical to investigate the financial condition of the operator in these cases. Investors should obtain current, independently-audited financial statements from these operators to determine their ability to honor their turnkey agreements. Smaller operators may not be able to compete with larger, more established and financially-secure major independent operators, and this could also affect well or lease operations.

Management Risk

As is the case with operators, management experience, or a lack thereof, can be a critical factor in the success of the venture. An inexperienced manager may lack the necessary knowledge about a proposed operator and the drilling prospect itself. Interested investors are advised to investigate whether or not the drilling program sponsor and the operator have professional in-house staffs to monitor and evaluate operations on a continual basis.

Disparity in Contribution Risk

In some oil and gas drilling programs, there is a disparity in contributions among the investors who put up cash, the program sponsors, and the operators. Many sponsors of drilling programs retain a carried working

interest or an overriding royalty interest in the program.

An entity with a carried working interest does not bear its proportionate share of the costs incurred during operations—i.e., the costs associated with the drilling and completion of a well. Owners of an overriding royalty interest bear no costs whatsoever—neither the costs incurred during operations nor the costs incurred after the well begins producing oil and/or gas in commercial quantities. Some operators also retain carried working interests for themselves. This results in overlapping participations that shoulder no portion of the costs of the operations, leaving more to be borne by the non-sponsor, non-operator investors.

Post-Production Risk

There are certain risks attendant to operations on a well, even after it is completed and producing in commercial quantities. Many wells must be re-worked and subsequent operations performed. This results in the need for an additional cash infusion by the working interest owners; thus, their investment may not be limited to their initial capital contribution.

Moreover, environmental risks do not end when a well starts producing. Environmental factors can hamper subsequent operations, and a working interest investor can remain liable for damages to persons or property even after he or she has sold his working interest in the well.

Duration Risk

The life of a working interest is limited. Working interest investors own an interest in the asset only for the period of the lease. The interest terminates with the expiration of the lease, and a new lease needs to be negotiated in order for the working interest positions to be retained. If the working interest was acquired through a 1031 exchange, the expiration of the lease could be a taxable event.

Liquidity Risk

Liquidity refers to the ability to convert an asset to cash, with little or no loss in value. Like real estate, working interests are not as liquid as some other assets. Although there is a strong secondary market for energy assets, you cannot expect to sell them in a day as you can a stock or bond. You need to allow for a reasonable period of time.

Summary

Numerous opportunities to invest in working interests are available, and many independents offer these ownership interests in their drilling programs. However, working interest investments are risky, especially for those investors who are not themselves in the industry and are relying on the performance of the operators. It is important for these potential investors to seek advice from industry professionals and do due diligence on both the operators and the investment itself.

Generally speaking, although working interests in oil and gas properties can be excellent investments with good returns, they may not be the best investment opportunity for the inexperienced energy investor. There are a large number of moving parts and associated risks, which are often not fully explained to the investor. Working interests are sometimes presented as being less risky than they really are, and the unwary investor is lured by the siren song of the high potential returns.

As discussed in this chapter, working interest owners remain jointly and severally liable long after they've sold their interest and stand to lose much more than their initial investment. In some instances investors have experienced dramatic losses, leading to a poor reputation for oil and gas investments in general. The good news is that there is an alternative ownership investment available in the oil and gas industry that has less risk while still offering investors the ability to earn income from domestic energy production: royalties. We cover the benefits and risks of this investment in the next chapter.

FIVE

inside energy royalty interests

W hat is a Royalty Interest? Most people have a general idea about what a royalty is. Essentially, a royalty is a payment made for the right to utilize the assets, intellectual property, copyright, or brand image of another. Royalty payments are common in the music industry, wherein recording artists are paid a royalty by the record label for the use of their songs. In the retail sector, franchisees make royalty payments to the franchisor for the use of its concept (intellectual property), brand, and products. In both instances, the royalties are ongoing and are typically based on a fixed percent of the sales.

Energy royalties are very similar. As discussed in the previous chapter, the oil and gas lease agreement stipulates that the working interest operator (lessee) pay the mineral rights/royalty interest owner (lessor) a royalty for the oil and gas produced on the leased acreage. The payment is established as a fixed percentage of the monthly gross revenue generated.

Also as mentioned in the previous chapter, royalty interest owners participate in all the production revenues, but bear none of the exploration, production or drilling costs and are indemnified from all liabilities associated with the process. There is a trade-off to being free of the risks associated with the venture, however. Royalty interest owners are considered to be passive investors. This means that they have no operational control and typically cannot influence when or where the operator drills wells in the future.

Characteristics of Mineral/Royalty Interests

The private mineral ownership right that exists in the United States is not enjoyed by the peoples of most countries; more often than not the mineral resources are government-owned, as noted in Chapter 4. The specific rights afforded owners of mineral estates in the U.S. include the following:

- The option to lease, convey or retain rights to all or a portion of the mineral deposits contained within the land from just below the surface to the center of the earth.

- The right to utilize the surface as reasonably necessary to explore, develop and transfer the minerals.

Some suggest that the ability of private citizens to lease and sell their mineral rights in a free market environment is one of the largest contributing factors to the current energy boom. The competition among oil companies for leaseholds on properties deemed to contain rich deposits serves to establish a market price for the acreage. Furthermore, the activities of these companies could ultimately enable the U.S. to reduce its dependency on foreign oil by replacing it with domestic production.

Advantages of Royalty Interest Ownership

As with any asset class, royalty interests have a number of advantages that make them attractive investments—not only for the large institutional investors, who are among the most active participants in this market, but also for individuals.

No Cash Calls

One of the biggest advantages of royalty interest ownership is that they are relatively expense-free assets. In contrast to working interest owners, who must pay their proportionate share of the ongoing expenses related to operating and maintaining the wells, the royalty interest owner shoulders none of these costs. While many lease agreements stipulate that royalty

interest owners must pay a share of the marketing and transportation costs associated with getting the product sold and delivered, the amount is usually deducted from the monthly payments.

Long-Term Income

Royalty interests offer the potential for decades of effort-free monthly income. As long as the well is producing, the royalty interest owners must be paid before the operator and other working interest owners can receive any part of the revenue generated. And investors in energy royalties are not responsible for any of the operational activities or decision-making; they simply sit back and receive their royalty checks. This makes the investment particularly well-suited for foundations, endowment funds, and individual investors with long investment horizons.

Real Assets

Real assets are tangible assets, such as real estate, fine art, equipment, and the whole range of commodities, which includes wheat, orange juice, precious metals, and oil and gas. Mineral and royalty interests also fall into this classification. Real assets have value in their own right, in contrast to financial assets like stocks and bonds, which are merely pieces of paper and/ or computer entries whose value lies in their claims on a real asset.

Low Correlation

Because real assets, in general, tend to have a low correlation with financial assets, they serve to reduce the risk of an investment portfolio that is largely comprised of financial assets. Mineral and royalty interests offer even greater diversification potential because the returns on these real assets are also unrelated to the trends in the real estate and credit markets. This makes them ideal instruments for 1031 exchange investors who have a large percentage of their investment monies in real estate.

Inflation Hedge

Historically, as the dollar weakens and its buying power is reduced, prices on commodities like gold, timber, and crude oil rise because they have intrinsic value; their value is not tied to the value of the currency. Increases in the prices of oil and natural gas result in higher selling prices for these products and bigger royalty checks for the mineral interest owners.

Passive Investment

Because mineral royalty interests are considered to be passive investments, the income generated is not considered to be "unrelated business taxable income" (UBTI) by the Internal Revenue Service. This allows the income to grow tax-free in retirement and other qualified accounts.

Serendipity

Since mineral interests can be held in perpetuity, the potential for the unexpected upside exists. New or increased production can result from a number of different factors:

- New drilling: If the operator chooses to drill new wells in the future, the working interest owners bear all the expenses and liabilities, while the royalty owners enjoy their fixed percentage of the new revenue stream.
- Technological advances: Technological advances are a common driver of upside potential. Most recently, the introduction of

(i.c.) horizontal drilling and hydraulic fracturing has opened up billions of dollars in reserves that were heretofore considered uneconomical to pursue.

- Enhanced recovery methods: Techniques such as waterflooding and CO_2 injection increase the pressure in the reservoir, extending the productive life of the wells.

- Unitizing or pooling of acreage: To maximize the efficiency with which an area is developed, state regulatory agencies may mandate that adjacent tracts in a specific area be treated as a unit since oil and gas can easily move through the rock below the surface from one tract to another. All the operators of the wells within a unit share all the expenses and revenues pro rata, based on their percentage acreage within the unit. The royalty owners enjoy the benefits of diversification. Rather than receiving royalties based on the production of one well on a small tract, they are entitled to a percentage of the revenue from all of the wells in the unit. Although this percentage is necessarily smaller than the percentage of the revenue a royalty interest owner would receive from the single well drilled on his own property, his risk of receiving no or low revenue as the result of a dry hole or marginal-producing well is reduced.

- Downspacing: State agencies establish the number of acres that must separate each well location. Many plays begin with 80-acre spacing; however, in the interest of maximizing recoverable resources, the state may increase the well density in the area if operators can demonstrate that wells may be developed closer to each other without impacting the recovery rates of the wells. This can exponentially increase the potential new well locations, to the benefit of the royalty interest owners. If an area with 80-acre spacing is downspaced to 20 acres, the number of potential drill sites in a standard 640-acre section increases from 8 to 32.

Risks of Royalty Interest Ownership

As attractive as mineral/royalty investments are, like any other investment they are not without risks. Each mineral position is unique and possesses both advantages and risks that are specific to it, and it is crucial for an investor to evaluate the distinctive characteristics of a particular interest prior to purchasing it. The most common risks associated with mineral and royalty interests are discussed below:

Pricing and Production

Although the royalty payment you will receive is a fixed percentage of the production revenue, the dollar amount of the payment is not fixed. It is dependent on the amount that was produced and sold, as well as the selling price. Oil and natural gas prices fluctuate daily, based on global market conditions. Production volumes depend on the development activity of the holdings and also vary from one month to the next. It is important to realize that because of these factors, the payments will always be variable.

Lack of Operational Control

While freedom from decision-making can be an advantage to royalty ownership, it can also be viewed as a disadvantage. Although mineral/royalty interest owners are not responsible for any expenses associated with the development and operation of a well, they also have no say in these matters. They cannot force an operator to drill any new wells once they have established a producing well.

Payment Delays and Lags

A characteristic of the oil and gas industry is the payment in arrears for production. There is always a lag between the production date and the revenue date; this is usually 60 days for oil and 90 days for natural gas. Too, when a mineral or royalty interest is acquired, the operator may suspend payments owed to the interest during the time it takes for the title to be recorded in the new owner's name. This is to ensure that payments are made to the owner of record at the time the production occurred. The suspended funds are released as a lump sum afterwards.

Policy Changes

The oil and gas industry is highly regulated. As such, it is always subject to policy changes that can impact production levels and/or commodity pricing. Likewise, changes in tax laws, including modifications to currently-allowed industry-related deductions, can affect the economics of development, thereby influencing royalty income.

Reserve Estimate

The amount of oil and gas that is economically recoverable for an interest can be estimated through engineering. These estimates attempt to forecast future production potential and are based on industry-standard evaluation techniques. Nevertheless, certain assumptions are made in order to arrive at an estimate. If any of these assumptions prove to be wrong, the amount in reserve could be more or less than forecasted. If less, the return on investment will be below expectations, and the value of the asset will decrease accordingly.

Liquidity

Like working interests, royalty interests are not as liquid as investments in most financial assets are. This means that you cannot expect to be able to sell these properties in a single day and will need to allow a reasonable period of time to divest yourself of these interests.

The Tax Treatment of Mineral and Royalty Interests

There are two categories of taxable income in the United States: ordinary income and capital gains income. Ordinary income includes salaries and wages and is taxed at a rate that is based on the income bracket of the taxpayer; the higher the income bracket, the higher the marginal tax rate, which is defined as the percentage tax paid on each additional dollar earned. Capital gain income is generated when a capital asset, like real estate or a mineral interest, is sold for a profit. Typically, long-term capital gain income is taxed at a lower rate than ordinary income, and a long-term capital gain is traditionally defined as a gain on the sale of a capital asset that has been held for more than 12 months.

But "typically" and "traditionally" are the operative words in that last sentence. Tax laws can and do change. There was a period of time when capital gains received no preferable tax treatment. And the definition of "long-term" has varied from 6 months to 18 months over the last few decades. Regardless, as discussed previously in this book, a 1031 Exchange can be used to acquire both working and royalty interests, thus deferring capital gains taxes. In this section, we will concentrate on the tax treatment of royalties received.

Royalty Income

Royalty income is treated as ordinary income for federal income tax purposes. This applies to both the advance royalty (aka the lease bonus) and the monthly royalty payments and means that this income is taxed at the marginal tax rate of the investor. In 2013, the highest marginal tax rate was 39.6%. This is the marginal rate paid by single filers with over $400,000 of adjusted gross income (AGI); the same rate applies to those married filing jointly taxpayers with over $450,000 in AGI. Most states also treat royalty income as ordinary income, but there are some noteworthy differences and, like federal tax laws, state tax laws can change, so it is best to consult with a tax advisor. At this writing state income tax rates range from 0 to 11%, depending on the state.

The taxes due on royalty income can be deferred if the mineral interest is held in a tax-deferred account, such as an Individual Retirement Account (IRA). As mentioned earlier in this chapter, one of the advantages of royalty interest income is that because it is passive income, it does not fall under the classification of "unrelated business taxable income" (UBTI), which would dictate that taxes be paid on the income received, even if the asset is held in an IRA or by an otherwise tax-exempt entity, like a charitable trust. Another advantage of passive income is that it is not subject to self-employment tax. While the working interest owners must pay self-employment taxes on the income they derive from the venture, royalty interest owners do not.

Depletion Deduction

If you are a real estate investor, you are probably familiar with the depreciation deduction you can take, which serves to reduce the amount of income on which you must pay taxes. Taxpayers with an economic interest in mineral property are entitled to a depletion deduction, which is similar to - albeit not exactly the same as - a depreciation deduction. It is noteworthy that the U.S. Supreme Court

ROYALTIES

has called this deduction "the single best business deduction" in the entire tax code.

The depletion deduction is shared between the lessor (mineral interest owner) and the lessee (working interest owner). There are two methods of calculating the deduction: the cost method and the percentage method, and the taxpayer is generally required to use the method that provides the greater deduction. *use best*

■ Cost depletion

The cost depletion allowance is based on the quantity of oil or gas produced during the tax year with respect to the estimated total recoverable reserves for the given well. Basically, the rate per unit is calculated by dividing the depletion basis of the property by the total recoverable reserves. That rate is then multiplied by the units sold during the tax year to arrive at the cost depletion deduction. The depletion deduction ceases once the adjusted basis of the well is zero dollars.

■ Percentage depletion

The percentage depletion allowance is calculated as a percentage of the gross income generated by the property during the year. The percentage depletion rate is 15% of the gross income provided by the well as long as the well's average daily production is less than or equal to the depletable quantity, which is set at 1,000 BOPD (barrels of oil per day) under current tax law. If your average daily oil production exceeds this amount, a couple of additional steps are necessary to calculate your deduction.

In contrast to cost depletion, percentage depletion can continue to be taken for the life of the well, even when the adjusted basis of the well is zero. However, there is a cap on the deduction allowed under the percentage depletion method. The maximum deduction that can be taken is the lesser of the following:

☐ 100% of your taxable income from the property, calculated before the depletion allowance is deducted, or

☐ 65% of your taxable income from all sources, again figured without the depletion allowance.

Bear in mind that excess depletion deductions can trigger the Alternative Minimum Tax (ATM). Designed to ensure that taxpayers pay at least some minimum amount of tax based on their income level, the AMT effectively eliminates the tax savings that certain deductions provide. It goes without saying that you should always consult with a professional tax advisor to determine the applicability of these taxes and deductions to your individual situation.

Maximize Your Deductions

Investors in real estate are well aware that depreciation is always subject to recapture and that a property can never be depreciated for more than its purchase price. So, consider the following question: If you own a fully depreciated property worth $400,000 free and clear and you exchange it for a replacement real estate property of equal value, how many new tax deductions will you get? The answer is "none." The basis of the original real estate—which is zero since it is fully depreciated—becomes the basis of the new property. However, if instead you exchange the real estate for a royalty interest of the exact same value, you will be entitled to claim an annual depletion deduction equal to 15% of the royalty income generated (in most cases)—and no recapture.

This strategy is most beneficial for real estate investors who own property that has been depreciated to a low or zero basis. By exchanging the real estate for energy assets, they can enjoy a tax deduction that they would not have had if they had exchanged the real estate for another piece of real estate. The 15% annual depletion deduction is like found money, adding more value and greater returns to the overall investment portfolio. This can and should be a deciding factor for the 1031 exchange investor.

Depleting Assets?

To be clear, oil and gas reserves are finite resources. Each barrel of oil that is produced is one less barrel available, and it is entirely possible that one day all the earth's oil will be completely exhausted. However, the methodology that is used to estimate reserves has, over time, been proven to underestimate what can actually be recovered. This discrepancy is what allows mineral and royalty interests to appreciate, even as the existing wells on the acreage are being depleted.

Proved Reserves vs. Undiscovered Resources

The Securities and Exchange Commission (SEC) requires publicly traded companies to provide reserves data, offering the following definition as a guideline: "Proved oil and gas reserves are those quantities of oil and gas, which, by analysis of geoscience and engineering data, can be estimated with reasonable certainty to be economically producible—from a given date forward, from known reservoirs, and under existing economic conditions, operating methods, and government regulations." In this context "reasonable certainty" is generally considered to be a 90% probability, based on data from currently producing wells. This methodology does not include future production outside of the producing area. Furthermore, it ignores the effects of future technological improvements and fails to consider any resources that may be produced in a higher pricing environment. Simply put, "proved reserves" are a very conservative estimate of available resources.

A much more expansive view of the resource base is provided by the United States Geological Survey (USGS) in what it terms "technically recoverable resources." These include "resources in accumulations producible using current recovery technology, but without reference to economic profitability." Since the mineral interest owns all of the sub-surface deposits within a particular acreage position, this method of evaluation provides a more accurate estimate of the resources of the mineral estate. Moreover, new technological developments can lead to an increase in the technically recoverable resources estimate, which is not the case for the SEC-defined proved oil and gas reserves.

The graphical illustration on the following page highlights the more conservative nature of the proved reserves estimate and also depicts how improved technology, such as horizontal drilling and hydraulic fracturing, can increase ultimate recovery:

The Opportunities

The possibility for underestimation of the underlying reserves can prove to be financially beneficial for the savvy mineral and royalty investor,

U.S. PROVED & UNDISCOVERED RESOURCES

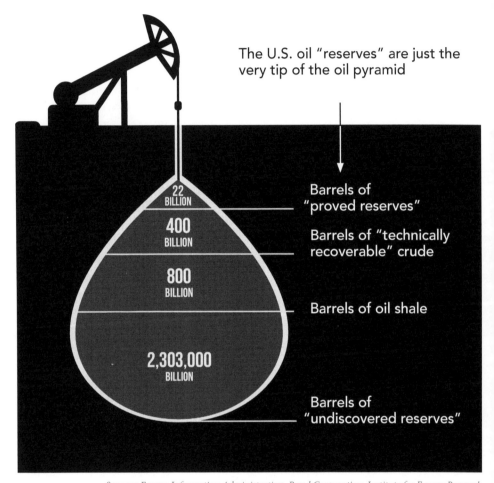

The U.S. oil "reserves" are just the very tip of the oil pyramid

22 BILLION — Barrels of "proved reserves"

400 BILLION — Barrels of "technically recoverable" crude

800 BILLION — Barrels of oil shale

2,303,000 BILLION — Barrels of "undiscovered reserves"

Sources: Energy Information Administration, Rand Corporation, Institute for Energy Research

providing long-term upside potential to properties that can actually appreciate in value as the reserve base grows.

Consider, for example, a couple of areas of the United States with lengthy production histories. The first commercial well in the U.S. was drilled in Titusville, Pennsylvania in 1859 in a production region called the Appalachian Basin. That area sits above the Marcellus Shale, which spreads across Pennsylvania, New York, and West Virginia and is estimated to contain more than 500 trillion cubic feet of natural gas. Once considered to be a drilling impediment, with technological advances the Marcellus Shale formation is now seen as a prototypical solution to the nation's energy problem. Yet another example is the Williston Basin in North Dakota, which began producing oil in the 1950s and is currently producing unprecedented volumes from the Bakken Shale. Some estimate that the Bakken Shale area could contain more than 10 billion barrels of oil. A perpetual mineral interest in either of these two areas could conceivably have already provided over half a century of royalty income for its owner while, at the same time, the underlying reserve base—and hence the value of the interest—continues to increase.

Of course, the best way to increase the growth potential of your investment in energy royalties is through diversification. A portfolio containing interests in multiple oil and gas producing regions offers more opportunity for reserve expansion. At the same time, diversification eliminates the unique risks associated with a solitary property, thereby aligning the growth rate of your portfolio with the overall domestic reserve growth rate represented in the EIA chart on the preceding page. Diversification is what, in my opinion, turns the distinctive characteristics of minerals and royalties into an attractive investment vehicle.

SIX

energy royalty interests for a 1031 exchange: putting it all together

You probably already know that if you buy a building on leased land - i.e., purchase an above-the-ground real estate interest- the building would qualify for a 1031 exchange. You may not realize that beneath-the-ground interests, such as mineral rights, are considered "like kind" properties and qualify for 1031 exchanges, as well.

A Bit of History

People began investing in oil and gas interests in the early 1900s and began executing tax-deferred, like-kind exchanges, as defined by the Revenue Act of 1921, in them as early as the 1940s. The 1921 Act was amended in 1954, and Section 1031 of the Internal Revenue Code (IRC) of 1954 established the basic rules that govern 1031 exchanges today.

In 1968, the Internal Revenue Service (IRS) created Revenue Ruling 68-331 to clarify and update Section 1031 of the 1954 Act. The ruling establishes that real estate ownership interests - whether above the ground, on the ground, or below the ground - meet the definition of "like kind" property, making such interests eligible for 1031 exchanges. In its discussion of Ruling 68-331, the agency stated that the exchange of a leasehold interest in a producing oil lease for a fee interest in a ranch would qualify for Internal Revenue Code (IRC) Section 1031 treatment. After this ruling, it became more common for investors to exchange "traditional" real estate for working or royalty interests in domestic oil and/or gas wells. A number of other rulings have confirmed that working and royalty interests are deemed to be real property in the eyes of the IRS, among them Revenue Rulings 55-526, 88-78, and 73-428.

Tips For Investing in Oil & Gas Royalties

As with any asset class, there are many factors that must be considered when investing in oil and gas royalties. My partners and I have acquired a multitude of royalty packages over the years for both our own portfolios and the portfolios of our various partnerships, funds, and clients. In the process, we have developed a set of 7 criteria on which we evaluate prospective purchases.

Clean Title

When executing a 1031 exchange, you must be exchanging like-kind property—in this case, real property for real property, as opposed to real property for personal property. Mineral interests are real property. As such, mineral interest ownerships (titles) are recorded in the courthouse of the county in which the interests are located. Interested investors should examine the document to ensure that the title is clean and that the party selling the mineral interest has a legal ownership position in it, just as they would if they were purchasing surface rights or a fee simple estate.

Long-term Reserves

In order to receive a long-term return on your investment, it is necessary to invest in wells with a long life. It's a very simple concept: the longer the reserve life, the longer the investment will pay out. Ideally, we would like to invest in wells that have been engineered by professionals who can verify at least 25 years of reserves. Practically speaking, it is usually too time consuming and cost prohibitive to hire the services of a professional engineering firm for an oil and gas property the size that most 1031 investors will require. Nevertheless, it is important to get an approximation of the reserve base in order to evaluate the investment potential of an interest.

The best way to do this is to mine the data that can be found on the websites of the larger operators. You will find information on a given area or play that they are drilling, along with production and reserves estimates and other technical information. Furthermore, these operators are usually publicly traded companies, and, as such, must file quarterly and annual reports with the U.S. Securities and Exchange Commission (SEC). They must also report on anything that could have a material effect on their stock price, e.g., the discovery of a rich oil field, at the time of its occurrence. These publicly-available documents offer a lot of details about the company's operations, and the financial statements and discussions thereof provide information about specific income-producing assets of the firm. You'll usually find these materials in the investor relations section of the company's website.

For example, clicking on the "Investors" tab on the ConocoPhillips' homepage (www.conocophillips.com) opens a menu of items, including "Investor Presentations," "Fact Sheets and Financial Information," and "Company Reports." The "Fact Sheets and Financial Information" provides an abundance of data, including the average net production of Oil, NGL, and Natural Gas in specific areas, and also briefly discusses ConocoPhillips' current focus areas, one of which is the Eagle Ford shale trend in south Texas. We learn that the company plans on drilling more wells in the area in 2013.

A click on "Company Reports" enables you to pull up ConocoPhillips' most recent annual report. In this document, Eagle Ford is said to be "one of the company's most promising resource opportunities." Later in the report, we learn that Eagle Ford increased its annual production by 144% in 2012, with 11 operated drilling rigs, and that it averaged 89 Million Barrels Oil Equivalent Per Day (MBOED) in the 4th quarter of the year. Updated information can be found in the company's most recent quarterly report. It can be accessed by clicking on "SEC Filings" on the sidebar under "Company Reports."

While every well and every section in a given play is not the same, the information you can obtain on a company's website will give you a general idea of what the operator expects from its investment in each well. This will help you calculate the estimated life and expected return of wells drilled in that area.

Diversity

You've probably heard the word "diversify" applied to traditional investments, such as stocks and bonds. It basically means, "Don't put all your eggs in one basket." In other words, don't invest all your money in one stock. The same concept applies to investing in mineral/royalty interests. Holding a diversified portfolio of these interests will maximize the benefits you can receive from investing in this asset class. You can seek diversity in 3 different ways:

1. Invest in a number of currently-producing wells. While investing in royalty interests of a single well for a 1031 exchange is certainly an option, you will be exposing yourself to unnecessary risk since that specific well may end up being a marginal producer, at best. Just as a mutual fund invests in a large number of stocks and a real estate investment trust (REIT) holds a number of different properties in order to minimize the total risk of their portfolios, investing in royalty interests of multiple wells will reduce your risk exposure and the volatility of your returns.

2. Invest in wells located in different areas. Geographical diversification is another way to seek diversity. This is accomplished by acquiring interests in multiple producing areas, just as you might seek to diversify a real estate portfolio by purchasing properties in a number of different localities. Investors executing 1031 exchanges should consider exchanging into an asset that is not concentrated in just one or two sections, but is instead diversified across many sections located in multiple counties and states. This reduces concentration risk and will give the investor ownership interests in assets with different production characteristics. Moreover, owning interests in more than one play reduces the risk of production interruptions due to forces of nature or unforeseen issues concerning the area.

3. Invest in wells with different operators. While royalty interest owners are not responsible for any expenses, they also have no say in the daily operations of a well. They must rely on the operator working interest owners to manage their assets properly. Many domestic operator working interest owners are large, publicly-held corporations. Owning royalty interests in wells operated by a diverse group of these well-financed, liquid companies is the best way to secure your returns. These large companies have the necessary resources to

continue drilling new wells. And they have the incentive to do so. As working interest owners, they enhance their own revenues by drilling new wells. Too, major operators are valued in the public markets in large part based on the reserves they hold, a value that is reflected in the price of the company's stock. Their businesses are focused on maintaining and/or increasing reserve levels, and the ability of a publicly-traded company to meet this challenge organically through the effective development of its leaseholds is critical to its economic success. These large operators are, therefore, motivated to spend their money to drill more wells, which, in turn, makes them ideal partners for the owners of the royalty interests.

Verified Production Volumes

It is important to research the production history of the asset in which you are considering investing in order to estimate its future production volume. The price of the commodity and the production volume of the asset are the two biggest determinants of the return, so a thorough analysis of the production data should be conducted.

You can obtain data from several sources, including the databases of some of the bigger oil and gas states, like Texas and Oklahoma. The primary sources for production data, however, are the sellers of the interests. This information is reported to them each month with the royalty checks they receive from the various operators. It is a good idea to request to see the check stubs, starting with the most recent and going back for as many months as possible to verify both ownership information and the production volume.

Underdeveloped Mineral Acreage

Recent advances in drilling techniques, specifically horizontal drilling and hydraulic fracturing, have opened up exploration opportunities in formations that were considered uneconomical to pursue just 5 or 10 years ago. Most of these formations are simply pay zones that are located farther below the surface in already established areas with decades of operating history. Many operators are now focusing on areas with multiple zones.

When you invest in energy royalties, you are investing in a depleting asset; all oil and gas wells will eventually run dry, even though it may take decades. The acquisition of all the mineral rights associated with the selling landowner's acreage is a critical component of a quality royalties investment.

The owner of the mineral rights to the land will always receive a fixed percentage royalty from any production as long as he owns the mineral rights to all depths, and, at the same time, is not responsible for any of the associated costs. Owning royalty interests on current production with the potential for future development extends the life of the investment, thus increasing the expected overall return.

Therefore, investors should try to identify areas in which operators have demonstrated that they will drill multiple wells. ConocoPhillips' stated intentions for the Eagle Ford shale trend in Texas that we used as an illustration earlier in this chapter is an example. While there is no guarantee that a company will drill a well in every section of the targeted area, you can get an idea of the potential for mineral owners of a given play. Our strategy is to purchase mineral acreage in these plays, focusing on sections with just one or two currently producing wells, with the hopes that additional wells will be drilled over time, offering new sources of income and increasing our reserve base—all at no additional cost to us.

Undeveloped Mineral Acreage

We recommend investing in undeveloped mineral acreage in addition to investing in underdeveloped acreage to further insure the long-term production potential of your royalty interest portfolio. Investing in mineral interests on acreage that is currently undeveloped but has been leased by a major operator is analogous to owning real estate in the path of progress.

Acquiring mineral interests "ahead of the drill bit" is more speculative than acquiring interests in existing production. When doing so it is important to understand the production profiles of the wells in the area and the general trends of the play. Acreage in the heart of the play, the "fairway," is typically more expensive than acreage on the periphery, but it is also more likely to be drilled.

 It is imperative to conduct due diligence on the operator of the acreage as well. Begin by researching the terms of the lease. The period of time that the operator has to drill on the acreage is called the primary term. This can be any length of time; we often see 3 years stipulated. Some lease agreements allow the operator to extend the lease beyond the primary term into a secondary term. Regardless, it is critical that you know when the lease will expire because if the operator does not drill at least one well on the acreage before that time, it will lose the lease.

Many operators prefer not to relinquish leased acreage, thus forgoing the ability to earn a return on the lease bonus that they paid on signing the lease agreement, but corporate strategy and economics play major roles in this decision. The operating tendencies, stated development plans, and financial status of the driller are key factors to consider when evaluating undeveloped mineral acreage.

Mineral interests in undeveloped mineral acreage are great complements to a portfolio of currently producing interests. For one thing, as might be expected, mineral interests in non-producing acreage in an area of aggressive development will cost less than they would if the acreage was producing. Additionally, each new well added serves to extend the production life of the assets in the portfolio, increasing the investor's expected return.

Detailed Supporting Documentation

The quality, accuracy, and detail of the supporting documentation is key in both the acquisition and liquidation of royalty assets. As a prospective purchaser, you need to obtain detailed revenue, engineering, and production data on a property. As a seller, you need to be able to provide this information.

Finding Energy Royalty Investments

As noted in previous chapters, mineral/royalty interest ownership is unique to the United States. The fact that mineral rights to the land are, for the most part, privately owned creates the opportunity for these assets to be bought and sold, and these transactions take place daily in the U.S. However, because of the general nature and size of mineral interests, the market in them is very fragmented. Unlike the real estate market, which is fairly efficient due to the fact that 95% of buyers and sellers use the Multiple Listing Service (MLS) to buy and sell homes, the energy markets don't have one central system or clearinghouse. Although recent technological advances are moving the energy sector in this direction, at the present time energy interests are generally acquired through one of four venues, as described below:

Aggregators

An aggregator is a person or group that continually acquires mineral/

royalty interests over time for a single portfolio or multiple portfolios. These groups are usually good sources from which to acquire diverse mineral holdings because they often carve out undivided interests in their royalty portfolios in order to obtain the capital necessary to purchase more royalties for further portfolio diversification. This makes them a good fit for a 1031 exchange investor because they can tailor the acquisition to match the investment amount that the investor requires to execute the exchange.

Oftentimes, a 1031 investor will have a problem finding an exchange asset equal in value to the property he is relinquishing, which leaves him with a deficit or a surplus. The acquisition amount flexibility offered by aggregators circumvents this issue. Moreover, aggregators usually retain an ownership position in the acreage they are selling; it is rare to see them liquidate a position entirely. The fact that the seller is maintaining an interest in the asset gives buyers the peace of mind of knowing that the seller believes in its profit potential.

The primary drawback of entering a transaction with an aggregator is that the individual or group may not have a verifiable track record. You need to ensure that the aggregator is reputable and has a past record of clean transactions.

Broker-dealers

You can also purchase energy royalties through some FINRA-registered broker-dealers. Sponsor businesses construct large portfolios of direct-title royalties and offer these for sale through select broker-dealers. As is the case with aggregators, these investments often provide the elements necessary for 1031 exchange investors. These are what are known as Regulation D offerings and, as such, must meet certain requirements of the U.S. Securities and Exchange Commission (SEC). In addition, they are vetted by the broker-dealers on a number of levels. The downside is that there are large loads (i.e., sales charges) attached to the offerings, resulting in lower-than-otherwise returns to the royalty interest investors.

Energy Exchanges/Auctions

Although there is not one central energy clearinghouse, clearinghouses do exist in the energy sector. As they evolve and mature, they, too, provide a venue for 1031 exchange investors. Currently, the two dominant players are Petroleum Listing Service (PLS) and Energynet.com.

PLS has been in existence since 1987 and provides the energy sector with the equivalent of real estate's MLS service. It also brokers and direct markets energy properties, including both working and royalty interests. Energynet.com is an online auction service that offers a continuous market in all types of energy assets, with bidding available 24/7/365. Investors have the opportunity to purchase and sell energy interests via a negotiated sale, a sealed bid, or an auction.

There are two downsides for 1031 exchange investors, however. First, the packages offered for sale on these platforms may not offer the flexibility needed. Typically, these are all-or-nothing sales. The sellers do not carve out undivided interests as is the case with aggregators, so the investor may not be able to match the value of the relinquished property. Second, the assets listed for sale on these venues may not fit the timelines required by Section 1031 of the Internal Revenue Code (IRC) as discussed in Chapter 2.

Examples of Royalty Offerings

To give you a better feel for the various types of offerings you can find in the market, we provide examples of recent listings from each of the outlets discussed in the previous section:

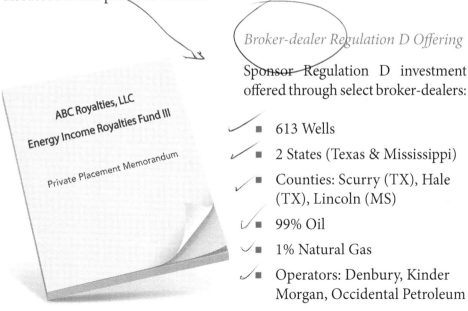

Broker-dealer Regulation D Offering

Sponsor Regulation D investment offered through select broker-dealers:

ABC Royalties, LLC
Energy Income Royalties Fund III

Private Placement Memorandum

- 613 Wells
- 2 States (Texas & Mississippi)
- Counties: Scurry (TX), Hale (TX), Lincoln (MS)
- 99% Oil
- 1% Natural Gas
- Operators: Denbury, Kinder Morgan, Occidental Petroleum

AGGREGATOR OFFERING EXAMPLE

Royalty Property For Sale
XYC Royalties, Inc., a privately held energy acquisition firm, is divesting a portion of its holdings of royalty, mineral and overriding royalty interests. Buyers will receive an undivided interest which will be conveyed in title and may be considered "like kind" replacement property for a 1031 exchange.

Price: up to $1,350,000

This package includes interests in two of the most active plays in North America:

Mississippi Lime (OK, KS)	Wattenberg Field (CO)
The Mississippi Lime formation stretches from northern Oklahoma into central Kansas. For decades this area has been developed using conventional drilling methods, but more recently has proven to be a prolific horizontal target. The centerpiece of Sandridge Energy's drilling program, the operator committed over $1 billion to the play in 2013. Sandridge is currently testing the potential for multiple production zones within the Mississippian formation, which could create additional drilling locations on this acreage in the future.	Located north of the Denver International Airport in the DJ Basin, the Wattenberg Field is in the early stages of a massive horizontal expansion by Anadarko Petroleum and Noble Energy. Noble Energy reports to spend $10 billion over the next five years to drill 2000 new horizontal wells in this play while Anadarko plans to be drilling 600 per year by 2016.

Package Highlights

- Current average annual yield ~10.4% based on recent 6 months' cash flow
- 300 Active Wells:
  - □ 75% Oil
  - □ 15% Natural Gas
  - □ 10% Liquids
- 3 states, 3 counties
- Prominent Operators: Noble Energy, Anadarko, Sandridge Energy
- 50+ drilling permits on the properties
- 500+ potential future drilling locations

Contact the seller for more information.

Aggregator Offering

The illustration on the previous page depicts what a typical aggregator offering might look like.

Energy Exchange Offering:

Oklahoma Royalty Package

- 127 Wells
- 1,500 net mineral acres
- Cana Woodford formation
- Counties: Canadian, Custer, Dewey, and Blaine
- Varying royalty interests available
- Average net cash flow: $38,400 a month

Contact the seller for more information.

SEVEN

a case for oil & gas royalties in a 1031 exchange

I n this chapter we will examine executing a 1031 exchange using real estate and energy royalties from a financial perspective. While neither I nor my partners are certified financial planners or licensed registered representatives, we have consulted with numerous people who are. They have shared their insights and expert advice on the subject with us, and we, in turn, are sharing it with our readers to provide a springboard for discussions between investment real estate owners and their own advisors.

The Realities of Real Estate Ownership

To begin, let's consider some of the basic facts about owning investment real estate. Although every property and every ownership situation is different, there are nonetheless some commonalities:

Active Management

Investment real estate ownership requires active participation and management. Real estate demands time and resources, whether periodically or on a daily basis. Although there are different management options, the bottom line is that the investor must deal with the infamous "tenants, toilets and trash" one way or another. And the day-to-day requirements are not getting any easier to fulfill; instead they are becoming more difficult in today's environment of increased litigation, regulation, and tenant demands.

Ongoing Capital Decisions

All successful real estate investors have one thing in common: they are savvy capital decision makers. The real estate market is far from static, and investors need to monitor the economic and business environments of the areas in which their real estate is located in order to determine how their properties can best compete within that specific region. They must make ongoing capital decisions in order to react effectively to changes in the market.

Capital Calls

Capital calls are one of the basic realities of real estate ownership. They can be the result of the terms of a loan, a catastrophic event, or just routine updates. All real estate, regardless of type, requires maintenance and improvement over time, and capital is needed to meet these demands. Some of the outlays necessary to replace or repair items, furnish space, complete projects, or update a property can be significant, and the investor must have the funds readily available.

Irregular Lending Cycles

The capital markets in the United States are well-defined and highly regulated. Nevertheless, they still run in unpredictable cycles based on many factors, including national and local economic environments and the general health of the business markets. Most investment real estate owners rely on borrowed funds, and the degree to which the capital markets are free or constrained at any given point in time can have a profound impact on their investments. If owners need capital and do not have enough in reserve, they can be severely hurt if they find themselves forced to borrow money in a constricted lending environment, such as the one that has existed in the U.S. in recent years.

Illiquid Assets

Although there is an organized and sophisticated secondary market for real estate - controlled mostly by commercial and residential real estate brokers - it is nevertheless an illiquid asset. Selling real estate is not only expensive, but it is also time-consuming. The process can take many months. Even the act of preparing a property for sale can be onerous. Careful planning and proper management is essential to maximize profits. An owner cannot expect a quick sale or turnaround of his property unless he is willing to sell it at a steep discount. Investment real estate owners usually do not hold their properties indefinitely. Decisions have to be made by the owners or their estates in order to transfer ownership and/or manage the assets as efficiently and effectively as possible.

Transitioning Real Estate to Heirs

Most commercial and investment real estate in the United States is held by the baby boom generation. Many baby boomers are either in or close to retirement and are faced with the decision of what to do with their real estate holdings and how to transition it to their heirs. If not handled properly, this can be a ticking time bomb for the beneficiaries. Let's revisit some of the facts about real estate ownership that we discussed in the previous section and consider their potential effects on the heirs.

Active Management

The majority of real estate beneficiaries have no real experience buying and selling these assets, let alone any knowledge about what is involved in property management. Inheriting real estate can prove burdensome to family members, and numerous heirs on the title can be a enormous source of friction. It is not uncommon for the value of a property to decrease when it becomes part of an estate because of improper management and general lack of attention.

Ongoing Capital Decisions

This is an area that can be problematic for beneficiaries for several reasons. Most importantly, as previously discussed, it takes a savvy decision maker to allocate the capital necessary for ongoing real estate management wisely. It is rare for a person who inherits real estate to have the same acumen as the previous owner, and this can adversely affect both the property value and the cash reserves with the passage of time.

Capital Calls

Real estate beneficiaries often misunderstand the ownership requirements or simply don't have the means to hold the property long term. Moreover, when the property is left to multiple family members, they may not all have the funds available or may not agree on the capital expenditures. It is a recipe for trouble when some parties want to allocate the capital while others do not or cannot. This can lead to long-term feuds and legal battles that ultimately result in the devaluation of the property.

Irregular Lending Cycles

If the beneficiaries do not have the capital reserves in place to manage the property and/or do not manage the reserves properly and they are faced with a constrained lending market, they may have no good available options.

Benefits of Energy Royalties

We covered the benefits of owning royalties in previous chapters. Below, we highlight some of the specific advantages that energy royalties have over real estate ownership and also address why these royalties may prove to be a better investment for your retirement years:

Potential for decades of monthly income

If an investor owns an interest in one or more producing wells in the U.S., he can reasonably expect that the well(s) will continue to produce for many years - perhaps even many decades. Once wells are online, they tend to follow a typical decline cure for that given area and continue producing until the hydrocarbons are exhausted. With the advances in technology a well or section can often be further developed in a cost-effective manner by the operator into new zones, thus extending the life of the asset out indefinitely. Mineral owners have the right to a fixed percentage of current and future production revenues from a defined acreage position. This provides an additional source of income, at no additional cost to the investor, which can be especially helpful to those preparing to retire.

No ongoing management

Mineral owners bear no responsibility for the drilling or operation of the well(s) on the property. The operator or driller leases the acreage and,

per the terms of the lease agreement, is responsible for all the drilling and continuing operations on every well on that property and must pay the mineral owner a royalty for everything produced and sold. The fact that this investment does not require active management is another feature that can make it more attractive than real estate to retirees.

No capital calls

The lease agreement between the operator and the mineral owner stipulates that the operator will incur all drilling and ongoing operating costs associated with the wells drilled on the property. Mineral owners are never responsible for these costs and can never be held accountable for them. The continuous capital calls that real estate owners must face can be unduly burdensome for retirees living on a fixed income.

No liability

Mineral owners do not bear any liabilities associated with drilling and operating a well on the property. These liabilities fall on the shoulders of the operator and other working interest owners. Real estate owners are liable for any damages to belongings or persons that occur on the property they own, including previously unknown environmental hazards. Retirees, in particular, may wish to be free of this burden.

Title to underlying mineral rights

As with real estate, mineral interests are held in perpetuity. Mineral owners can sell all or a fraction of their interests at any time without the approval of any other entity, including the operator of the wells on the property. They can assign title to anyone they choose.

Uncorrelated with real estate markets

Oil and natural gas prices have historically been uncorrelated with domestic real estate prices. This means that their addition to a real estate portfolio can reduce the investor's risk exposure, making them an ideal choice for investors seeking diversification.

Annual tax deduction

Revenue from energy royalties are entitled to an annual depletion deduction of no less than 15%. This means that no more than 85% of the income received from royalties is taxed. The deduction can be taken indefinitely, even after the property has a zero basis. Retirees in higher tax brackets will especially appreciate this.

Combining Energy with Real Estate to Achieve Your 1031 Exchange Needs

One of the most difficult elements of executing a 1031 exchange is matching the value of the new acquisition to that of the property being disposed. Truly equal exchanges are rare. Typically exchangers either have to come to the closing table with cash or fall short of the amount for which they sold the relinquished property, thereby exposing themselves to capital gains tax and recapture fees.

COMMON EXCHANGE SCENARIO

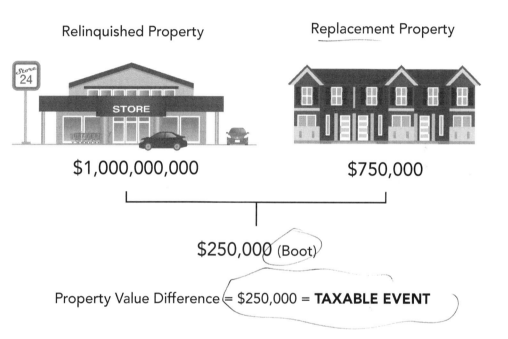

Relinquished Property

Replacement Property

$1,000,000,000

$750,000

$250,000 (Boot)

Property Value Difference = $250,000 = **TAXABLE EVENT**

Energy royalties can provide a way to make a clean, even exchange. In most cases, an energy royalty is an undivided interest in the minerals; that is, it is not usually an interest in a specific well or restricted to a small corner of the section on which wells are located, but rather an interest in the whole section or multiple sections.

This allows an acquisition to be structured to fit the dollar amount needed for an even exchange. The buyer will still own the same asset insofar as the whole section (or multiple sections) is concerned, but he will own more or less of it, depending on the amount he requires to effect an equal exchange.

In the example below, the exchange is made whole, triggering no taxable event, by using the energy royalties as a "fill in" for the shortfall of $250,000 when the $1,000,000 retail investment property is exchanged for the multi-family property. The energy royalty asset can remain the same, regardless of the amount of "fill-in" needed; a smaller (or larger) undivided interest is acquired to fit the requirements. For example, if the price of the multi-family property had been $800,000 instead of $750,000, the investor would have needed to purchase only $200,000 of the energy asset; and if the price of the multi-family property had been $600,000, the investor would have needed to purchase $400,000 of the energy asset.

NEW EXCHANGE SOLUTION

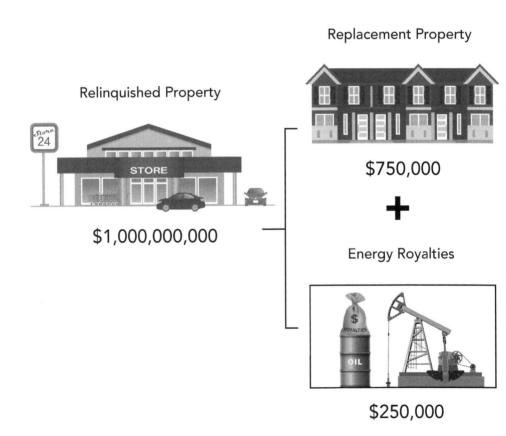

Replacement Property

Relinquished Property

$750,000

+

$1,000,000,000

Energy Royalties

$250,000

Property Value Difference = $0 = **NO TAXES**

In our experience, this is how energy royalties are most often used. They provide a unique, yet very effective, way to satisfy an exchange. It resolves the problem most real estate investors face when executing a 1031 exchange and eliminates the need for them to bring more money to the closing. Moreover, the resulting portfolio is more diversified, containing both real estate and energy assets—and this was accomplished with a single transaction.

Summary

While investment real estate has a number of benefits, there are aspects of this asset class that make it less conducive for certain types of investors. Specifically, an investor's heirs may lack the interest and/or knowledge and capital qualifications necessary to continue to manage the decedent's real estate portfolio effectively. And because real estate is an illiquid asset, they may have a difficult time disposing of the properties.

Retirees may no longer wish to devote the time and money necessary to manage their real estate interests. Furthermore, they may no longer have the funds available to meet the capital calls that are a reality of real estate ownership. Many may welcome the opportunity to shed the liability burden that property ownership entails.

Energy royalties offer a number of advantages over real estate ownership, including the potential for decades of monthly income, with no effort or additional investment needed. They also provide the investor with an annual tax deduction. And because oil and gas prices tend to be uncorrelated with real estate prices, their addition to a real estate portfolio reduces the investor's risk exposure and gives more diversity. This can be easily accomplished via a 1031 exchange, a nontaxable event. In fact, energy royalties can solve the value-inequality problem faced by investors executing 1031 exchanges by filling in any shortfalls.

EIGHT

the importance of owning
domestic reserves

lthough a lot of people don't realize it, we are currently in the midst of a renaissance in the energy industry that is changing the world as profoundly as the invention of the combustible engine. Those of us who study the industry closely are well aware of it, though, and recognize that what we are witnessing today will impact all aspects of modern life. In this chapter I will present some of the details regarding the recent resurgence and discuss what I believe the future holds in order to give you an appreciation for what's happening.

The Past Decade

As few as 10 years ago most industry experts believed that the world's energy supply, which consisted mainly of oil, natural gas, and coal, had peaked. Vertical drilling was the primary method used to extract these hydrocarbons, but in many cases even a series of very successful vertical wells could remove only a small portion of the reserves in a given formation—often less than 10%. While the majority of geologists agreed that there were still large amounts of reserves in the ground, the consensus was that there was no real practical or cost-effective way to extract them from the earth and get them to market. Metaphorically speaking, energy companies were plucking all the low-hanging fruit from the oil and gas trees. The commonly-held belief was that this low-hanging fruit was dwindling and we would someday--relatively soon--run out of it. This was definitely a scary thought, given that energy is the driving force in the world's industrialized nations, as well as the most important element for emerging countries.

Enter U.S. ingenuity and the nation's provision for private ownership of energy resources. Horizontal drilling and multistage hydraulic fracturing were employed in the Barnett Shale play in north Texas in the late 1990s, leading the domestic oil and gas industry down a path that would forever change the way energy sources are exploited. While the two methodologies used were not new to the industry, their application in hard rock, shale formations was. Shale is a fine-grained sedimentary rock that can be a rich source of petroleum and natural gas, but shale formations were difficult to access and were mostly avoided due to many unsuccessful attempts at extracting the hydrocarbons using conventional vertical drilling methods. Horizontal drilling combined with multistage hydraulic fracturing proved to be a cost-effective way to drill for hydrocarbons in areas that the experts never before believed were reachable.

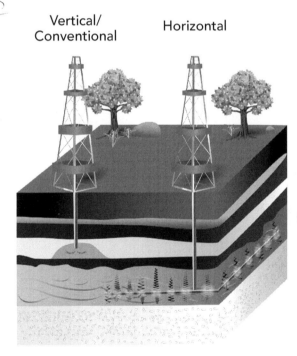

DRILLING METHODS

Vertical/Conventional   Horizontal

The Renaissance

The success of the Barnett Shale venture led to a natural gas drilling frenzy in the lower 48 states. Using the lessons and methods learned, aggressive drilling in large shale formations in other parts of the country, including

Louisiana, Arkansas, and West Virginia, commenced. Private ownership of the land and mineral interest in these regions enabled operators to push forward at as fast a pace as their capital would allow since they were not impeded by any government red tape. In essence, private citizens, partnered with oil and gas companies, reversed a 30+ year trend of declining energy production in the U.S.

These rewarding enterprises resulted in an enormous surge in the supply of natural gas—unlike ever before in the United States. For the first time in recent history, the supply of natural gas exceeded demand, forcing the price of the commodity to a 20-year low. The lower selling price, in turn, made drilling in these plays uneconomical once again: the costs of doing so outweighed the benefits—i.e., the revenues that could be generated.

The genie, however, was out of the bottle. The domestic oil and gas companies had learned new hydrocarbon drilling techniques, and they applied this newfound knowledge to target other formations, such as oil shale and other liquid plays. As these large, well-capitalized firms expanded their drilling operations into other regions of the U.S., huge quantities of hydrocarbons were unearthed in North Dakota, south Texas, and Colorado.

In addition to entering new areas, operators also utilized the new methodologies in older, more conventional plays, which allowed them to extract more from these areas than they previously thought was economically feasible. Mature fields in west Texas and several parts of Oklahoma were targeted, and unexplored zones in those areas yielded huge reserves of oil. Now realizing that anything was possible, operators in different areas competed fiercely to lease up as much acreage as possible to add to their inventories. Capital was allocated for leasehold positions at an unprecedented pace.

After the land was leased up, the companies began drilling aggressively, using cost-effective, fruitful techniques. For the first time in many years, industry observers believed that the United States could become energy independent by the end of the decade. By all accounts, the nation appears to be on schedule to do just that as these operations continue at full thrust.

How Long Can It Last?

Prior to the discovery of the aforementioned new drilling techniques, domestic oil production had been declining steadily for several years, beginning in the late 1970s. The low-hanging fruit in the United States had been plucked, and major energy companies began allocating more and more of their resources overseas in an effort to maintain their current levels of reserves. The first material increase in U.S. production didn't occur until 2009 when the domestic output grew by 10%, reversing a 23-year downward trend. Industry experts, along with Wall Street and Washington, are now wondering, "How long can it last?" In mulling over this question, let's consider some of the currently-known facts regarding the recoverable reserves, new formations, multiple zones, and hydrocarbon mining.

U.S. CRUDE OIL PRODUCTION

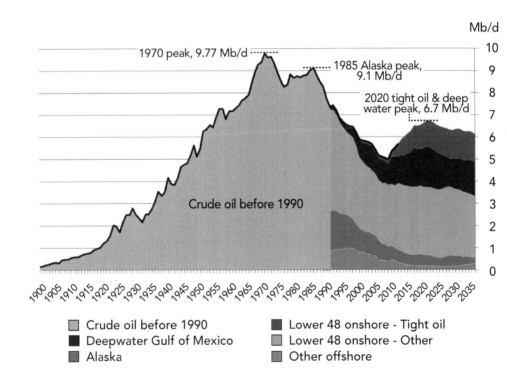

Mb/d

- 1970 peak, 9.77 Mb/d
- 1985 Alaska peak, 9.1 Mb/d
- 2020 tight oil & deep water peak, 6.7 Mb/d

Crude oil before 1990

⬜ Crude oil before 1990	⬛ Lower 48 onshore - Tight oil
⬛ Deepwater Gulf of Mexico	⬜ Lower 48 onshore - Other
⬛ Alaska	⬜ Other offshore

Domestic Reserves

The Energy Information Administration (EIA) is the statistical arm of the U.S. Department of Energy. As such, its mission is to collect, analyze, and disseminate "independent and impartial energy information to promote sound policymaking, efficient markets, and public understanding of energy and its interaction with the economy and the environment." A summary of salient facts taken from recent reports by the agency on domestic natural gas and oil reserves is presented below:

Natural Gas

The three largest unconventional shale formations discovered as of January 1, 2009—the Barnett, Haynesville, and Marcellus shales—had total recoverable reserves of 259 trillion cubic feet (TCF) of gas. Recoverable reserves in these 3 formations have increased every year for the last 5 years.

These formations alone provide 9 to 10 years of the demand for gas at the current consumption level of approximately 80 billion cubic feet (BCF) of gas per day, and they are not the only reserves in the nation. Moreover, total domestic natural gas reserves have been on the rise for the past 13 consecutive years. Total proved reserves in the U.S. on December 31, 2010 were 317.5 TCF. In 2011, reserves increased by almost 10% to 348.8 TCF.

Oil

The three largest oil shale plays in the nation as of January 1, 2009—the Bakken, Eagle Ford, and Niobrara plays—had recoverable reserves of 9.7 billion barrels of oil. Total domestic proved reserves of crude oil amounted to 25.2 billion barrels on December 31, 2010. Like natural gas reserves, crude oil reserves have also been increasing. By December 31, 2011, proved reserves of crude oil had increased by 15% to 29 billion barrels. This was the 3rd consecutive annual increase and the highest recorded volume of proved crude oil reserves since 1985. The U.S. consumes about 17.5 million barrels of oil per day.

In summary, these statistics demonstrate that our domestic reserves of both natural gas and crude oil have turned the corner and are now on the rise after declining steadily for several decades.

New Formations

While the formations underground are by no means new, the ability to drill into them is. This is a direct result of the ability of U.S. operators to implement new methodologies successfully. Operators can now move up and down a formation in a cost-effective way, productively targeting several different zones using newfound technologies. Not all operators employ the exact same methods, but basically they all drill multiple horizontal wells within a given section—usually defined as 640 acres. And some operators are now drilling several wells into different formations or zones in a given section utilizing just one drilling pad. This allows them to extract more hydrocarbons with greater efficiency and less cost.

Multiple Zones

To illustrate the point, let's look at just one of several areas in the country where this is happening – in the well-established Permian Basin of west Texas.

As is the case in many areas within energy-producing regions, there exists multiple layers or zones containing exploitable hydrocarbons, as seen in the graphic below.

MULTI-WELL DRILLING

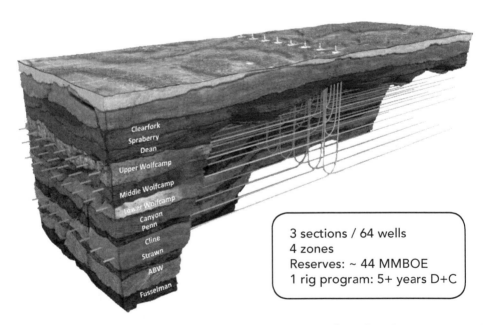

Clearfork
Spraberry
Dean
Upper Wolfcamp
Middle Wolfcamp
Lower Wolfcamp
Canyon
Penn
Cline
Strawn
ABW
Fusselman

3 sections / 64 wells
4 zones
Reserves: ~ 44 MMBOE
1 rig program: 5+ years D+C

Source: Laredo Petroleum Company Prentation

The Spraberry and Dean formations shown closer to the surface have been productive for more than 70 years, mostly through conventional vertical wells. Recently, new technology and the advancements made in horizontal drilling techniques have opened up the deeper zones, in this area the three Wolfcamp formations (upper, middle and lower), and the Cline formation located more than a mile below the surface. The development plan shown here will use eight drilling sites in a 1,920 acre unit (1 mile x 3 miles) to drill 64 wells into the four deep formations.

As the exhibit on the previous page illustrates, several formations are stacked on top of each other. Operators establish drilling plans that utilize horizontal drilling to tap into multiple zones. They continue to work to refine their methods to minimize costs while maximizing the production from these multiple sources. These lower formations are not new discoveries; they were just not cost-effective to pursue when vertical drilling was the industry status quo. Enhanced horizontal drilling methodologies and multi-stage hydrologic fracturing, coupled with rising energy prices, have made drilling these plays economically viable.

Mining For Hydrocarbons

You'll sometimes hear a seasoned oil and gas person say that the industry as it is today is unrecognizable. They reflect on the "old days," when drilling for hydrocarbons was an exciting, risk-taking endeavor. Although good companies back then employed solid science and experienced professionals to analyze formations, it was still a "wildcat" game, and just about every well could end up being a gusher or a dry hole. Both the risk and the reward were huge.

Such is not the case today. Advancements in science and technology have changed the game to a large degree. Dry holes have become rarities because most of the wells drilled by mid-size and large operators today are horizontal wells. By the time the bit is put in the ground, the zone or zones they are targeting have been accurately pinpointed by using sophisticated technology and seismic data, and by drilling horizontally, the operator is assured of hitting pay dirt. While they can never be certain how much a well will produce, the margin of error is significantly smaller than it ever has been. Barring some type of mechanical malfunction, they know that they will extract something from the earth with every well drilled.

The domestic operators today are, more or less, hydrocarbon miners. They lease thousands of acres of minerals in various plays and "mine" the oil and gas, drilling multiple wells in each section. Because they have a significantly more accurate estimate of what each zone can produce, they patiently remain in an area, using their resources to drill into the various zones. They target the richer zones first, knowing that in time, they will return to the others. This makes them more closely resemble coal mine companies than the energy and power companies of old.

How Royalty Ownership Can Be Advantageous

Perhaps the most compelling reason to own domestic mineral/royalty interests - and a key point of this book - is that your ownership position is perpetual. As long as the land continues to produce, you continue to receive an income stream. And, as noted in earlier chapters, unlike working interest owners, royalty owners are not responsible for any of the operating expenses, nor are they liable for any costs associated with the drilling. Thus, new wells drilled on the land cost the royalty owner nothing, yet he receives his proportionate share of the revenue that each and every well generates.

As mentioned previously, most experts agree that there is still an immense amount of oil and gas beneath the earth both in the U.S. and abroad, just waiting to be tapped. The question is, and always has been, can we extract it in a cost-effective way? A bet on U.S. ingenuity has always been a good bet, and this has held true in the oil and gas industry, as evidenced by the recent developments and advancements that we've been describing.

When you own a mineral interest in a region that has been producing hydrocarbons, it is highly likely that there are more in the ground to be extracted than what has already been removed. They may be trapped in shale rock or some other type of challenging formation, or they may reside in deeper zones, but there are almost surely more hydrocarbons underground. Because of the demand for these energy sources and the ingenuity of American operators, the probability that they will eventually be extracted and taken to market is high. And, as the mineral owner, you have no out-of-pocket costs—only the potential for income.

What About The Alternatives?

Prior to investing in any venture, it is wise to examine the competition. In this case, the primary competitors are alternative energy sources. If one (or more) of these sources becomes abundant, is relatively cheap, and the American public believes its benefits outweigh the associated costs, it could usurp the position that oil and natural gas enjoy as primary sources of energy. If this were to happen, the prices of oil and gas could be expected to fall due to the diminished demand, and the lower selling prices might make it economically unfeasible for operators to continue drilling on the land in which you own a mineral/royalty interest.

Thus far, these alternative sources pose no threat. If you do some investigating, you will discover that many companies in alternative energy industries are aggressively lobbying for state and federal subsidies. They need money from the government to support their operations because the investing public is not yet sold on these alternatives. The projected returns over the next decade or two are not significantly high enough to entice investors to risk their monies. This could, of course, change if oil and gas prices increase to the point that American consumers begin looking more closely at the alternatives, and the demand for them increases accordingly. To date, however, the only people who have gravitated towards the alternative sources have been the politicians. To provide you with a clearer picture of the situation, a brief discussion of the pros and cons of these alternative energy sources follows:

Ethanol

The use of ethanol as an alternative energy source has been the subject of some heated debates in recent years. Proponents argue that it is a cleaner burning fuel than gasoline, and because it is made from corn, it puts more money into the hands of the American farmer, which is generally viewed as a positive thing. The USDA projects that over the next decade about 36% of the corn grown in the U.S. will be used in the production of ethanol.

But there is another side to the story. Not only is corn one of the basic ingredients in a lot of our foods, it is also used to feed our nation's livestock, and there is a finite amount of suitable farmland in our country. This means our supply of corn is necessarily limited. Ethanol production has increased the demand for the crop, causing both the price of corn and the cost of prime farmland in the Midwest to skyrocket in recent years. American consumers have felt the effects both in their grocery bills and when ordering a nice, juicy tenderloin at their favorite restaurant.

There is also the fact that ethanol is expensive—both to produce and to use. Ethanol production uses a great deal of energy, and unless the process improves, producing it in large quantities could very well be an energy net loss. Too, ethanol-based fuel tends to be more expensive than gasoline and doesn't offer the same fuel efficiency. Moreover, there is substantial evidence that this corn byproduct reduces the fuel efficiency in engines and that its use has resulted in engine corrosion in cars. Boaters complain that it corrodes fuel tanks and blocks filters.

The fact that ethanol has not gained popularity with the American consumer, combined with the fuel's high production costs, has found ethanol producers lobbying our nation's lawmakers for subsidies on the basis that they are offering a cleaner energy source, but are not yet realizing the profits necessary to support their operations. A law that created tax subsidies for the industry expired in January 2012, but the subsidies, in essence, continue, due to the Renewable Fuel Standards Mandate, which sustains a certain level of demand for the product. Nevertheless, until a more energy-efficient means of production is developed and the other issues are resolved, ethanol is very unlikely to replace oil as a primary energy source.

Nuclear Power

Nuclear power also has a footprint on the energy landscape of the United States. According to the U.S. Energy Information Administration (EIA), there were 65 nuclear power plants located in 31 different states at the beginning of 2013, with 104 nuclear reactors. Nuclear power plants have

provided 20% of the nation's annual electricity needs since 1990.

While the initial cost to build a nuclear power plant is substantially high, and there are processing and maintenance costs to consider, nuclear energy is considered by many to be a cost-competitive alternative energy source. However, the probability that any new plants will be built any time soon is very low. Although it may be economically viable, nuclear power is simply not politically viable. Details of the 2011 Fukushima Daiichi nuclear disaster are still fresh in people's minds. Property values around nuclear power plants often suffer, and no one wants a new nuclear power plant built close to his neighborhood. To propose the construction of one would be political suicide.

Too, there are those who disagree that nuclear power is a cost-effective energy source. They argue that while nuclear reactors may, at first glance, seem to provide a cheaper way to generate electricity than the use of oil, gas, and some of the other alternative energy sources, the analysis ignores some very important factors. For one thing, disposing of the nuclear waste is very expensive, in addition to being a major environmental problem. Secondly, basic construction and maintenance costs have increased significantly over the past decade or so. Add recent terrorism concerns and the need to build in extra security because of this, and the costs escalate even higher. The construction cost of a new plant is now estimated to be in excess of $1 billion. This last fact alone can prevent nuclear power from being a feasible dominant source of our nation's energy since the costs would have to be recovered through higher electricity prices.

Moreover, even a single terrorist attack--successful or not--on one of our country's existing nuclear power plants would effectively close the doors on nuclear power as an acceptable alternative energy source for years to come. Given the public's fears regarding the security of our nuclear facilities and the potentially adverse health and environmental impacts, it is very unlikely that nuclear power will supplant oil and natural gas as a dominant source of energy any time soon, if ever.

The Sun And The Wind

Harnessing the sun and the wind to supply our energy needs is aesthetically appealing. Solar and wind power are clean, renewable sources of energy, and perhaps at some point in the distant future, one or both will become economically viable. But the world is not close to having the technology to make either of these a reliable, cost-effective energy source at the present time.

While the earth's sun is said to be capable of providing 100% of the world's electricity requirements, we have not yet developed the means to

gather and store this energy on a large enough scale. In order to utilize solar energy when the sun isn't shining, e.g., at night or on a cloudy day, we need to be able to store it. Furthermore, the land needed to provide enough space to house the solar cells necessary to generate the same annual energy output as our nuclear power plants--about 8% of the total energy production in the U.S.--would be the size of the state of West Virginia.

According to the Institute for Energy Research, although the electricity capacity of solar energy has increased significantly since 1997, solar energy still only accounts for 0.1% of the net electricity generated in the U.S., putting it in last place among all the renewable energy sources. Technological advancements that will reduce the size of solar panels while simultaneously increasing their energy capacity are needed before solar power can ever become a significant source of energy. Research and development continues in this area, largely supported by federal government subsidies, but recent, well-publicized bankruptcies of a couple of these taxpayer-backed companies may prove to be a setback for the industry, impeding future progress.

The wind is an even more intermittent source of energy than the sun. While we know what the normal daylight hours are in a given area, the wind is unpredictable and inconsistent. Because of this, it is not a dependable energy source and requires supplementation by other sources. Wind turbines also require a lot of space in order to provide a reasonable supply of energy, and a lot of people consider them to be an eyesore. Those who reside close to these wind farms complain about the noise generated by the turbines. Many feel these negatives outweigh the positives of wind power, making it impractical as a primary source of power.

Conclusion

The recent innovations in drilling have increased the total returns that mineral interest owners can expect. Although alternative energy sources exist that could offer competition to the oil and gas industry, thereby reducing these potential returns, each alternative poses some serious problems that prevent it from being a threat for the foreseeable future.

NINE

parting words

A
t the time of this writing, the real estate markets have been experiencing a "correction" in many areas of the country following a very difficult period. Credit market failures put a lot of pressure on the real estate markets in the U.S., resulting in an extended period of depressed property prices. It is now clearer than ever that long-term strategies are essential for investment real estate owners--especially those in the baby boom generation who are nearing their retirement years. Predicting the future and/or attempting to guess when the real estate market has either peaked or bottomed out is very difficult, if not impossible. Common sense and long-term planning is the best approach.

Most investment professionals and advisors recommend diversifying your investment portfolio in order to minimize your risk exposure. This is especially important as you approach retirement. Unfortunately, diversification often requires the sale of an asset and the purchase of another, a transaction that can subject you to capital gains taxes. Our current federal tax code provides very few tax breaks for individuals, and this is particularly true concerning capital gain income. The answer to this dilemma lies in *The 1031 Solution*.

A 1031 exchange is an excellent way for a real estate investor to diversify his portfolio since capital gains taxes are deferred. And owners can execute multiple 1031 exchanges until the day they die. Moreover, when that day comes, their heirs will benefit from a stepped-up basis on the property (or properties) and will pay no capital gains taxes. But it is essential that real estate owners understand all the available options when electing to do a 1031 exchange. This tax code allows real estate to be exchanged for other categories of real assets, increasing the diversification potential even more. The objective of this book has been to inform you of these other options and explore one of them—energy royalties—in detail.

Our country is in the midst of an "Energy Renaissance." Technological advances have literally reversed a multi-decade decline in oil and gas production in the U.S. As the drill-out continues to move the country toward energy independence, more and more mineral owners will benefit from the royalties they receive from these new wells. Real estate investors can use the information and strategies outlined in this book and begin to examine energy investments as a means to transition from active to passive ownership of a real asset. And because the prices of oil and gas are uncorrelated with real estate prices, they will be diversifying their risk at the same time.

My goal in writing this book has been to encourage you to think outside the box and consider your investment alternatives, energy being one. As every wise investor knows, you should evaluate your options regularly, and you can now use this book as a valuable resource when doing so. There are many fine professionals who are knowledgeable about both 1031 exchanges and energy royalties. I encourage all my readers to work with a professional who is familiar with the available 1031 exchange options to design a long-term strategy that meets their individual needs. Reaping the benefits of all of the time, money, energy, and risk that are inherent elements of real estate investing can be a rewarding experience. However, there comes a time in our lives when we may want a more hands-off, passive experience. My hope is that this book helps each of you find a way that is a little less taxing (pun intended).

APPENDIX

glossary

GLOSSARY

1031 accommodator   A qualified intermediary who assists the exchanger to effect a tax-deferred exchange. Also described as a facilitator, a qualified intermediary cannot be the taxpayer, a related party, or an agent of the taxpayer.

1031 exchange   When capital gains tax is deferred in the exchange of "like-kind" property pursuant to Section 1031 of the U.S. Tax Code.

adjusted basis   Generally speaking, in a standard purchase of real property the adjusted basis is equal to the purchase price plus capital improvements less depreciation. Transactions involving exchanges, gifts, and probates and the receipt of property from a trust can have an impact on the calculation of the property's adjusted basis. The taxpayer's CPA or tax advisor is the party to look to for these types of questions.

arm's-length transaction   A transaction between parties who do not have a particular or special relationship that may affect the price level. The transaction is presumed to be between unrelated parities, each acting independently.

basis   The method of measuring investment in property for tax purposes. Calculation: Original cost, plus improvements, minus depreciation taken. Please contact your tax advisor for a complete analysis.

beneficiaries   1) One that receives a benefit. 2) The recipient of funds, property, or other benefits, as from an insurance policy or will.

boot   To the extent that investors do not exchange even or up in value and/or exchange even or up in equity and debt, they will have received non-qualifying property ('boot") in the exchange. If boot is received, tax is computed on the amount of gain on the sale or the amount of boot received.

broker/dealer   A firm that recommends, offers, or sells investments to the public that is required to be registered with the SEC, an SRO (Self Regulatory Organization), and the state securities divisions in every state in which the firm operates and in which the customer resides.

capital gain   Generally speaking, this is the difference between the sales price of the Relinquished 1031 Exchange Property less selling expenses and the adjusted basis of the property.

capital gains tax   Tax assessed on a capital gain. For most people, the capital gains tax rate is currently 15% if the elapsed time between purchase and sale is more than one year, and their normal tax rate if the elapsed time is 1 year or less.

cash-on-cash returns   This is the rate of return realized on the amount of equity (cash) invested. It is calculated by taking the income received from the property, adding the realized price appreciation during a specified period of time, and dividing by the cost of the investment. If the asset is not sold during the time period, it is the income receiv from the property divided by the cost of the investment.

charitable remainder trust	An arrangement in which property or money is donated to a charity, but the donor (called the grantor) continues to use the property and/or receive income from it while living. The beneficiaries receive the income and the charity receives the principal after a specified period of time. The grantor avoids any capital gains tax on the donated assets, and also gets an income tax deduction for the fair market value of the remainder interest that the trust earned. In addition, the asset is removed from the estate, reducing subsequent estate taxes.
	While the contribution is irrevocable, the grantor may have some control over the way the assets are invested and may even switch from one charity to another (as long as it's still a qualified charitable organization). CRT's come in three types: a charitable remainder annuity trust (which pays a fixed dollar amount annually), a charitable remainder unitrust (which pays a fixed percentage of the trust's value annually), and a charitable pooled income fund (which is set up by the charity, enabling many donors to contribute).
charitable trust	A charitable trust is a trust established for charitable purposes. Charities may take the form of charitable trusts, companies or unincorporated associations.
complete exchange	The process in which the replacement property is bought and all the respective paperwork is completed. This process is also known as the "replacement" of the exchange process.
constructive receipt	Although investors do not have actual possession of the proceeds, they are legally entitled to the proceeds. The money may be held by an entity

serving as the investor's agent or by someone else who has a fiduciary relationship with them. This creates a taxable event.

cost basis The initial value of an asset for tax purposes, usually calculated as the purchase price plus any capital improvements less depreciation. This value is used to determine the capital gain, which is equal to the difference between the asset's cost basis and the current market value.

decline rate The drop in oil or gas production rate over a period of time.

deduction An expense subtracted from adjusted gross income when calculating taxable income, such as for state and local taxes paid, charitable gifts, and certain types of interest payments. Also called tax deduction.

depletion deductions A tax deduction allowed by the IRS on income received from domestic oil and gas investments.

depreciation The deductible portion of improved real estate, as allowed by the IRS.

depreciation recapture The IRS currently taxes all excess depreciation taken on a property at 25% upon the sale of the property except when the tax is deferred using a 1031 exchange.

direct deeding Transfer of title directly from the 1031 Exchanger to Buyer and from the Seller to Exchanger after all necessary exchange documents have been executed.

disclosure (A) Prior to participating in a public offering of a direct participation program, a member or person associated with a member shall have reasonable grounds to believe, based on information made available to him by the sponsor through a prospectus or other materials, that all material facts are adequately and accurately disclosed and proved a basis for evaluating the program. (B) In determining the adequacy of disclosed facts in (A), a member or person associated with a member shall obtain information on material facts relating at a minimum to the following, if relevant in view of the nature of the program: (i) items of compensation; (ii) physical properties; (iii) tax aspects; (iv) financial stability and experience of the sponsor; (v) the program's conflict and risk factors; and (vi) appraisals and other pertinent reports. (C) For purposes of (A) or (B), a member or person associated with a member may rely upon the results of an inquiry conducted by another member or members, provided that: (i) the member or person associated with a member has reasonable grounds to believe that such inquiry was conducted with due care; (ii) the results of the inquiry were provided to the member or person associated with a member with the consent of the member or members conducting or directing the inquiry; and (iii) no member that participated in the inquiry is a sponsor of the program or an affiliate of such sponsor.

downleg property

The original or sold property being exchanged for the new or upleg property.

due diligence

The process of verifying that material facts and risks that could affect the outcome of an investment are disclosed. Due diligence is the responsibility of the broker/dealer and registered securities brokers/ representatives prior to offering investments to their clients. In a best-practices context, a thorough due diligence should be completed on each investment prior to offering the investment to investors.

economies of scale Economies of scale refers to the synergies that arise when large quantities of a product are traded. These advantages are usually price-related.

equity Equity is the amount of an investor's own money that is invested. The proceeds from the sale of a property might constitute some of the equity investment, but not necessarily all of it.

equity investment The portion of the total cost of the project that is not covered by debt financing.

escrow 1) Documents, real estate, money, or securities deposited with a neutral third party (the escrow agent) to be delivered upon fulfillment of certain conditions, as established in a written agreement. 2) An account held by the lender into which a homeowner pays money for taxes and insurance.

estimated ultimate recovery (EUR) The total volume of oil or gas that is expected to be extracted from a reserve. This projection is typically considered by oil sector analysts as a key indicator for investment in a petroleum or gas company.

exchange agreement The written agreement defining the transfer of the relinquished 1031 Exchange Property, the subsequent receipt of the replacement 1031 Exchange Property, and the restrictions on the exchange proceeds during the exchange period.

exchange period The period of time in which replacement 1031 Exchange Property must be received by the 1031 exchanger; ends on the earlier of 180 calendar days after the relinquished 1031 Exchange Property closing or the due date for the Exchanger's tax return. (If the 180th day falls after the due date of the 1031 exchanger's tax return, an extension may be filed to receive the full 180 day exchange period.)

exchange property   The property that an investor purchases when executing a 1031 exchange.

exchanger   The property owner(s) seeking to defer capital gains taxes by effecting a Section 1031 Exchange. (The Internal Revenue Code uses the term "Taxpayer.")

exchanging up   To accomplish a fully tax-deferred 1031 exchange, the investor needs to exchange even or up in value and exchange even or up in equity and in debt.

fair market value   The likely selling price as defined by the market at a specific point in time.

FINRA   Financial Industry Regulatory Authority (formerly NASD). FINRA is the result of a merger of the NASD and the regulatory arm of the NYSE that was completed the end of July 2007.

gain   1) An increase in value, as of an asset. Opposite of loss. 2) The amount of an investor's proceeds that is considered capital gain income for tax purposes. This gain is calculated as the proceeds from the sale of the security minus the cost of the security, including most charges.

ground lease   A lease in which only the land is rented. Also called a land lease.

identification period   A maximum of 45 calendar days from the relinquished 1031 Exchange Property closing that is allowed to identify potential replacement 1031 Exchange Property.

illiquid   That which cannot quickly and easily be converted into cash, with little or no loss in value.

installment note   An installment note is a form of promissory note calling for payment of both principal and interest in specified amounts, or specified minimum amounts, at specific time intervals. This periodic reduction of principal amortizes the loan.

institutional investors   Investors such as banks, insurance companies, trusts, pension funds, foundations, and educational, charitable, and religious institutions.

internal rate of return (IRR)   The internal rate of return is a measure of the worth of an investment. The internal rate of return is the interest rate that makes the present value of the investment's income stream equal zero. If the risk of the two investments is equal, the higher the internal rate of return the better the investment.

internal revenue service (IRS)   The federal agency responsible for administering and enforcing the Treasury Department's revenue laws, through the assessment and collection of taxes, determination of pension plan qualification, and related activities.

investment security   A security purchased for investment purposes, rather than for resale to customers.

irrevocable trust   A trust that cannot be altered, stopped, or canceled. Under circumstances wherein the trustee cannot interpret or carry out his or her specific duties, the court is asked to make legal determinations.

leverage   1) The degree to which an investor or business is utilizing borrowed money. Companies that are highly leveraged may be at risk of bankruptcy if they are unable to make payments on their debt; they may also be unable to find new lenders in the future. Leverage is not always bad, however; it can increase the shareholders' return on their investment and there are often tax advantages associated with borrowing. Also called financial leverage. 2) What the debt/equity ratio measures.

like-kind (property)   To qualify as like-kind property in a 1031 Exchange, the property must, by its nature, be real estate and not personal property. All investment real estate can be exchanged for real estate and qualifies as like-kind. Raw land for improved property is like-kind, and vice versa. Like-kind refers to the type of property being exchanged. Investors can exchange any real estate investment for any other type of real estate investment. For example, vacant land can be exchanged for rental property. In most cases, a personal residence is not like-kind investment property.

like-kind exchange   An exchange of similar business or investment assets, on which gains may be tax-deferred.

liquid   Easily convertible to cash with little or no loss in value. Opposite of illiquid.

living trust
A trust created during your lifetime. It is revocable, which means it can be amended or terminated anytime while you are competent. It is legally referred to as a revocable inter vivos trust. The trust becomes irrevocable upon your death. A living trust is used primarily to avoid probate and manage property. It does not save taxes.

loan to value (LTV)
The percentage of the property value borrowed (loan amount/property value = loan to value ratio).

master lease
A primary lease that controls subsequent leases and that may cover more property than subsequent leases.

mineral deed
Transfers ownership of the royalty interest, including the right to execute leases and receive bonus payments.

mineral rights
The ownership of the minerals under the ground. The owner of mineral rights has the right to drill and collect proceeds generated by all wells on such land. The owner of a mineral interest also has the right to execute leases and collect bonus payments. The mineral owner receives an up-front bonus from producing wells. The owner of mineral rights receives income from the production of oil and gas on such property.

mortgage boot
This occurs when the Exchanger does not acquire debt that is equal to or greater than the debt that was paid off on the relinquished 1031 Exchange Property sale; this is referred to as "debt relief." This creates a taxable event.

national association of realtors (NAR)	The national association for real estate professionals located in Washington DC that educates, organizes, and lobbies for the interest of realtors.
negative leverage	The use of debt financing, wherein the return on equity is reduced because the rate of interest on the debt is higher than the free and clear rate of return on equity.
net operating income	The sum derived after deductions from gross income for vacancy and other operating expenses by deducting vacancy and other operating expenses from gross income.
net sales proceeds	Proceeds from the sale of an asset or part of an asset, less brokerage commissions, closing costs, and legal and marketing expenses.
non-recourse	A loan wherein the lending bank is entitled only to repayment from the profits of the project the loan is funding, not from other assets of the borrower.
original basis	The purchase price of a property plus any closing costs associated with the purchase. It is used to calculate the capital gain or loss for tax purposes.
overriding royalty interests (ORRI)	A lease to receive the oil production proceeds from a well. Similar to mineral rights ownership, but different in that the royalty interest owner cannot execute leases and does not collect an up-front payment from producing wells. The owner of overriding royalty interests receives regular income from the producing well. Unlike mineral interests, the owners of royalties do not own the minerals under the ground, but only a portion of the profits from oil and gas production. Once the lease expires, overriding royalty interests expire.

passive income	Income derived from real estate or business investments in which the individual is not actively involved, such as a limited partnership.
passive investment	A real estate or business investment in which the investor is not actively involved in the day-to-day management activities.
passive investor	An investor who does not play an active role in the business.
personal property	Personal property is any property, tangible or intangible that is not land or affixed to land.
positive leverage	The use of debt financing that increases the return on equity because the rate of interest on the debt is lower than the free and clear rate of return on equity.
private annuity trust (PAT)	Enables the owner(s) of highly appreciated assets, such as real estate, a business, collectables or an investment portfolio, to be sold without incurring current taxation.
private letter ruling	Written decisions by the Internal Revenue Service in response to taxpayer requests for guidance. Some private letter rulings are published as a public Revenue ruling; however, most are only available to the public through IRS disclosure procedures. See 26U.S.C. § 6110.
private placement	A private placement is the sale of securities directly to a limited number of investors. Does not require SEC registration, provided certain conditions are met.

private placement memorandum (PPM)

A document that is prepared by the Sponsor that offers the investment. A PPM discloses the facts of the property, terms of the investment offering, and potential risks associated with an investor's participation in the investment.

pro rata

"In proportion to."

qualified intermediary (QI)

The entity that facilitates the exchange for the Exchanger. The term "facilitator" or "accommodator" is also commonly used, although the Treasury Regulations specifies the term "Qualified Intermediary." The entity who facilitates the exchange, defined as follows: 1. not a related party (i.e. agent, attorney, broker, etc.); 2. receives a fee; 3. receives the relinquished 1031 Exchange Property from the Exchanger and sells to the buyer; 4. purchases the replacement 1031 Exchange Property from the seller and transfers it to the Exchanger. Asset Preservation, Inc. (API) is a "Qualified Intermediary."

real property

In general, land and everything growing on it, attached to it, or erected on it. Examples of real property are single-family rental houses, apartments, shopping centers, office buildings and mineral and royalty interests.

realized gain

Refers to a gain that is not necessarily taxed. In a successful exchange, the gain is realized but not recognized and therefore not taxed.

recapture

The amount of tax to be paid on the difference between book value and sales price. The tax rate on recapture is 25%.

recourse
The right of a lender or holder of a note secured by a mortgage to look to the personal assets of the borrower or endorser for payment should the note be defaulted on, not just to the property assets itself.

registered representative
An individual who recommends or offers investments in return for a commission. A registered representative must be associated with a broker/dealer and registered as a securities professional with an SRO and all states in which he or she conducts business.

regulation D offering (Reg-D)
The sale of securities that meets the requirements established in Regulation D of the 1933 Act, which is not deemed to be made a public offering of securities. Regulation D provides an exemption from the registration requirements of a public offering of securities.

real estate investment trust (REIT)
Real Estate Investment Trust. An investment company that invests in income producing real estate and/or real estate related assets, such as mortgages.

relinquished property
The property sold by the Exchanger. This is sometimes referred to as the "exchange" property or the "downleg" property.

replacement property
The property acquired by the Exchanger. This is something referred to as the "acquisition" property or the "upleg" property.

royalties
Percentage paid to royalty owners for profit made from production of the land (i.e. oil, gas, minerals, hydrocarbons, etc.).

royalty

The share of production or revenues retained by government or freehold mineral rights holders.

safe harbors

A set of Treasury regulations that assist Qualified Intermediaries in tax-deferred exchanges so they can be sure that no constructive receipt issues will be encountered to disqualify the exchange.

Securities and Exchange Commission (SEC)

Securities and Exchange Commission. The primary federal regulatory agency for the securities industry, whose responsibility is to promote full disclosure and to protect investors against fraudulent and manipulative practices in the securities markets. The Securities and Exchange Commission enforces, among other acts, the Securities Act of 1933, the Securities Exchange Act of 1934, the Trust Indenture Act of 1939, the Investment Company Act of 1940 and the Investment Advisers Act. The supervision of dealers is delegated to the self-regulatory bodies of the exchanges. The Securities and Exchange Commission is an independent, quasi-judiciary agency. It has five commissioners, each appointed for a five-year term that is staggered so that one new commissioner is being replaced every year. No more than three members of the commission can be of a single political party. The Securities and Exchange Commission is comprised of four basic divisions. The Division of Corporate Finance is in charge of making sure all publicly traded companies disclose the required financial information to investors. The Division of Market Regulation oversees all legislation involving brokers and brokerage firms. The Division of Investment Management regulates the mutual fund and investment advisor industries. And the

Division of Enforcement enforces the securities legislation and investigates possible violations.

securitization

The process of aggregating similar instruments, such as loans or mortgages, into a negotiable security.

security

1) An investment instrument, other than an insurance policy or fixed annuity, issued by a corporation, government, or other organization which offers evidence of debt or equity. The official definition, from the Securities Exchange Act of 1934, is: "Any note, stock, treasury stock, bond, debenture, certificate of interest or participation in any profit-sharing agreement or in any oil, gas, or other mineral royalty or lease, any collateral trust certificate, pre-organization certificate or subscription, transferable share, investment contract, voting-trust certificate, certificate of deposit for a security, any put, call, straddle, option, or privilege on any security, certificate of deposit, or group or index of securities (including any interest therein or based on the value thereof), or any put, call, straddle, option, or privilege entered into on a national securities exchange relating to foreign currency, or in general, any instrument commonly known as a 'security'; or any certificate of interest or participation in, temporary or interim certificate for, receipt for, or warrant or right to subscribe to or purchase, any of the foregoing; but shall not include currency or any note, draft, bill of exchange, or banker's acceptance which has a maturity at the time of issuance of not exceeding nine months, exclusive of days of grace, or any renewal thereof the maturity of which is likewise limited." 2) Property which is pledged as collateral for a loan.

shelter	Invest (money) so that it is not taxable.
shut-in royalty	Payment to royalty owners under the terms of a mineral lease that allows the lessee to defer production from a well capable of producing in paying quantities but shut-in for lack of a market or marketing facilities.
simultaneous/concurrent 1031 exchange	When the Exchanger transfers out of the Relinquished 1031 Exchange Property and receives the Replacement 1031 Exchange Property at the same time.
sponsor	A real estate provider who sources the investment property, garners the financing, and manages the assets for the owners. Sponsors provide the service of packaging the investment property into a TIC format, allowing fractional undivided interests in one property to be sold to multiple co-owners as TIC interests.
starker	Name of the taxpayer in U.S. Court of Appeal's case that authorized Delayed Exchanges. The term a "Starker Exchange" is no longer used to describe a Delayed Exchange.
start exchange	The process in which the relinquished property is sold and all respective paper work for that process is completed. This process also know as the "relinquishment" of the exchange property.
step up in basis	The change in the value of an asset inherited upon the owner's death. The taxable gain is calculated based on the fair market value at the time of death, not the fair market value at the time the asset was purchased.

stepped-up basis   A common variation of step up in basis. See step up in basis.

subscription agreement   An application by an investor to join a limited partnership. In most cases, the investor will have to fill out a form created by the general partner evaluating the investor's suitability for the investment in the partnership. Notes: All limited partners must be approved by the general partner. Being a limited partner rather than a general partner is an attractive option since it means the investor's liability is limited to the amount he or she has invested in the partnership.

surface owner   Landowner who does not own mineral rights under his land. Surface Owner has the right to cultivate the land and build structures on the surface (houses, farms, ranches, etc.).

syndication   1) The combination of persons or firms to accomplish a joint venture of mutual interest. 2) The process of acquiring and combining equity investment from multiple sources.

tax credits   Tax benefits, granted for engaging in particular activities, that are subtracted on a dollar-for-dollar basis, from taxes owed.

tax deduction   An expense subtracted from adjusted gross income when calculating taxable income, such as for state and local taxes paid, charitable gifts, and certain types of interest payments. Also called deduction.

tax-deferred exchange   The procedure outlined under Internal Revenue Code Section 1031 involving a series of rules and regulations that must be met in order to take full advantage of deferring capital gains tax on the sale of investment real estate. §1031 tax-deferred exchanges are also commonly known as: Starker exchanges, delayed exchanges, like-kind exchanges, 1031 exchanges, section 1031 exchanges, tax-free exchanges, nontaxable exchanges, real estate exchanges, real property exchanges. Though all of these terms refer to the same thing, the most common term used today is tax-deferred exchange.

tenant

An individual or business that has possession of and pays rent for real estate owned by another party (called the landlord).

tenant in common (TIC)

The undivided fractional interest in an entire property wherein co-owners share in their portion of the net income, tax shelters, and appreciation. Each TIC owner receives a separate property deed and title insurance for his portion of the property investment.

time value of money

The difference in the value of cash received (expended) now versus its value if received sometime in the future.

transfer tax

A tax assessed by a city, county or state on the transfer of property that may be based on equity or value. The use of direct deeding in an exchange avoids additional transfer tax.

triple-net lease

A property lease in which the lessee agrees to pay all expenses that are normally associated with ownership, such as utilities, repairs, insurance and taxes. Also called closed-end lease.

trustee

An individual or organization which holds or manages and invests assets for the benefit of another. The trustee is legally obliged to make all trust-related decisions with the trustee's interests in mind and may be liable for damages for failure to do so. Trustees may be entitled to a payment for their services, if specified in the trust deed. In the specific case of the bond market, a trustee administers a bond issue for a borrower and ensures that the issuer meets all the terms and conditions associated with the borrowing.

turnkey
A product or service which can be implemented or utilized with no additional work required by the buyer (just by 'turning the key').

underwriting
The process by which investment bankers raise investment capital from investors on behalf of corporations and governments that are issuing securities (both equity and debt).

unleased mineral interest
Mineral rights that are not leased.

umbrella partnership real estate investment trust (UPREIT)
In the typical umbrella partnership real estate investment trust (UPREIT), the partners of an existing partnership and a newly formed REIT become partners in a new partnership termed the operating partnership. For their respective interests in the operating partnership (units), the partners contribute the properties from the existing partnership and the REIT contributes the cash proceeds from its public offering. The REIT is typically the general partner and majority owner of the operating partnership units.

wildcat drilling
The process of drilling for oil in an area that has been left unexplored.

working interest   Percentage share in well proceeds granted to the lessee of a property to explore for and to produce and own oil, gas or other minerals. Working interest owner bears the exploration, development, and operating costs on either a cash, penalty or carried basis.

RESOURCES

sources, references &
recommended reading

SOURCES & REFERENCES

- Internal Revenue Code (IRC)
- IRC § 1031
- U.S. Securities and Exchange Commission (SEC)
- United States Geological Survey (USGS)
- Paleontological Research Institute
- U.S. Energy Information Administration (EIA)
- Conoco Phillips
- Texas Railroad Commission
- Oklahoma Corporation Commission
- North Dakota Industrial Commission – Dept. of Mineral Resources
- Financial Industry Regulatory Authority (FINRA)
- Petroleum Listing Service (PLS)
- EnergyNet
- The Oil and Gas Asset Clearinghouse
- Multiple Listing Serviced
- SandRidge Energy
- Anadarko Petroleum
- Laredo Petroleum
- U.S. Department of Energy
- U.S. Department of Agriculture
- Institute for Energy Research
- CME Group (NYMEX)

RECOMMENDED READING & RESOURCES

American Petroleum Institute	www.api.org
Baker Hughes	www.bakerhughes.com
CME Group (NYMEX)	www.cmegroup.com
Department of Energy	www.energy.gov
Federation of Exchange Accommodators (FEA)	www.1031.org
International Energy Agency	www.iea.org
National Association of Realtors	www.realtor.org
National Association of Royalty Owners (NARO)	www.naro-us.org
North Dakota Department of Mineral Resources	www.dmr.nd.gov
Oil and Gas Investor	www.hartenergy.com
Oklahoma Corporate Commission	www.occeweb.com
Paleontological Research Institute	www.museumoftheearth.org
PLS	www.plsx.com
Rigzone	www.rigzone.com
Schlumberger	www.glossary.oilfield.slb.com
Texas Railroad Commission	www.rrc.state.tx.us
U. S. Energy Information Administration	www.eia.gov
U. S. Geological Survey	www.usgs.gov
U. S. Internal Revenue Service	www.irs.gov